WINNING WITH PEOPLE
WORKBOOK

Discover the People Principles that Work for You Every Time

JOHN C. MAXWELL

NELSON IMPACT
A Division of Thomas Nelson Publishers
Since 1798

www.thomasnelson.com

Published by Nelson Impact, a Division of Thomas Nelson Inc., P.O. Box 141000, Nashville, Tennessee, 37214.

Nelson Impact books may be purchased in bulk for educational, business, fundraising, or sales promotional use. For information, please email SpecialMarkets@ThomasNelson.com.

Published in association with Yates & Yates, LLP, Attorneys and Counselors, Orange, California.

ISBN: 0-7852-6090-0

Printed in the United States of America

05 06 07 08 09—5 4 3 2 1

CONTENTS

The Trust Question—Can We Build Mutual Trust?

The Investment Question—Are We Willing to Invest in Others?

The Synergy Question—Can We Create a Win-Win Relationship?

ACKNOWLEDGMENT

I want to say thank you to Kathie Wheat for her work converting *Winning With People* into workbook format, and for her years of exceptional work as a researcher, editor, and assistant.

INTRODUCTION

W hat does it take to win with people? Does an individual have to be born with an outgoing personality or a great sense of intuition to succeed relationally? When it comes to people skills, are there haves and have-nots, and we just have to accept whatever abilities God has given us? Can someone who is good at building relationships become even better?

Most of us can tell instantly when we're in the presence of a real "people person." Individuals with excellent people skills connect with us easily, make us feel good about ourselves, and lift us to a higher level. Our interaction with them creates a positive experience that makes us want to spend time with them.

Some people are so skilled at working with people that they ought to be in a relationship hall of fame. People such as Dale Carnegie, John Wooden, Ronald Reagan, and Norman Vincent Peale easily come to mind. Likewise, there are people whose relational abilities could make them candidates for a relational hall of *shame*. Leona Helmsley, Henry Ford (Sr.), Frank Lorenzo, and Dennis Rodman have such reputations.

But you don't have to read the paper or study history to find examples of relational extremes. You have to deal with them in your own life every day: on the street, at church, (perhaps at home), and certainly at work.

IT ALL STARTS WITH PEOPLE

All of life's successes come from initiating relationships with the right people and then strengthening those relationships by using good people skills. Likewise, life's failures can usually be traced back to people. Sometimes the impact is obvious. Becoming entangled with an abusive spouse, a crooked partner, or a codependent family member is going to cause great damage. Other times the trouble is less dramatic, such as alienating a coworker that you must interact with every day, failing to build a positive relationship with an important client, or missing key opportunities to encourage an insecure child. The bottom line is this: *most people can trace their successes and failures to the relationships in their lives.*

When I think about my personal failures, I can trace most of them to specific individuals in my life. I once picked the wrong person for financial advice and went into an oil deal with him. It cost me $10,000, which had taken my wife, Margaret, and me a long time to save. Another time I started a business and asked a friend to take charge of it, thinking he could make it go. But my judgment was poor, and after just a couple of years, the business was more than $150,000 in the red.

I'm not playing victim and blaming my failures on others. Rather, I'm saying that my interaction with others is a huge part of the process. In a similar way, I can't take credit for my successes. None of them was a solo endeavor. My interaction with others helped me to be successful. For every achievement, I can look back and see a relationship that made it possible. Without the help of people like Elmer Towns, Peter Wagner, and Jack Hayford, my career never would have gotten this far. Without the help of a whole slew of people at Thomas Nelson and at my company, the INJOY group, my book *The 21 Irrefutable Laws of Leadership* never would have been a million seller. And most of my financial blessings can be credited to the help and advice of my brother, Larry Maxwell, and my friend Tom Phillippe.

As important as relationships are professionally, they're even more critical personally. My spiritual life can be traced back to my relationship with my father, Melvin Maxwell. The reason I feel fulfilled every day can be attributed to my relationship with my wife, Margaret; she helps me enjoy our successes. And I must give credit for life itself to my relationships with others. If I hadn't met cardiologist John Bright Cage, I wouldn't be writing this right now. The heart attack I suffered in December 1998 probably would have killed me.

More than an Add-On

Have you ever found yourself dealing with someone difficult and thought, *She's talented, but she sure is hard to work with,* or *He's brilliant, but he doesn't seem to get along with anybody?* Such people never reach their full potential because they are able to accomplish only a fraction of what they could if they knew how to win with people. They don't understand that good relationships are more than just the icing on the cake in life. They *are* the cake—the very substance we need to live a successful and fulfilling life.

So what are people to do if they don't possess great relational skills? I must admit relationship building comes naturally to me. I was born a people person. But I've also worked hard to improve my skills. I've learned a lot of things about others and myself in half a century. And I've translated those ideas into twenty-five People Principles that *anyone* can learn. The most introverted individual can learn them and become more of a people person. And someone with a knack for people can become a master relationship builder.

I say that because these People Principles work every time. They apply whether you are young or old, sanguine or melancholic, male or female, employed or retired. I've practiced them for decades, and I've seen them work as I've traveled to dozens of countries on six continents. By following these principles, I've optimized my chance for success with others, and I've built positive, healthy relationships that have brought me professional success and personal satisfaction.

As you read and learn these People Principles, you will see that some of them are common sense. Others may surprise you. Perhaps you may question a few as a bit too optimistic. But I can tell you from experience, they really do work. One People Principle does not a relationship guru make. But practicing all of these principles will improve your life. (And you can be sure that you will never be nominated for the Relational Hall of Shame!)

That doesn't mean you will have a successful relationship with every person you meet. You can't control another person's response to you. All you can do is make yourself the kind of person others want to know and with whom they can build a relationship.

In life, the skills you use and the people you choose will make or break you. I've divided the People Principles in this workbook according to five critical questions we must ask ourselves if we want to win with people.

1. Readiness: Are we prepared for relationships?

2. Connection: Are we willing to focus on others?

3. Trust: Can we build mutual trust?

4. Investment: Are we willing to invest in others?

5. Synergy: Can we create a win-win relationship?

Learn and practice the People Principles, and you will be able to answer each of these questions in a positive way. That will make you relationally successful. You will be able to build healthy, effective, and fulfilling relationships. And you have a chance to become the kind of person who makes others successful, too. What could be better than that?

THE READINESS QUESTION
ARE WE PREPARED
FOR RELATIONSHIPS?

The most useful person in the world today is the
man or woman who knows how to get along with other people.
Human relations is the most important science in living.

—STANLEY C. ALLYN

I spent the first twenty-six years of my career as a pastor. I know of no other profession as demanding or intense when it comes to working with people. Individuals in ministry are called upon to lead, teach, coach, counsel, and comfort people at every age and stage of life, from the cradle to the grave. We're with them during many of the most joyful moments of their lives, such as the day they marry. And we're called upon during their darkest hours, such as when they try to save a marriage from a painful divorce, experience a child's tragic death, or look for answers as they face their own imminent death.

Over the years, I learned quickly to recognize people who were struggling relationally. They came in all ages, shapes, and sizes. Sometimes when I was counseling an unmarried person who just couldn't seem to get a relationship to work, he would lament about being alone and how much he wanted to get married. The sad thing was that instead of focusing on getting married, some people should be working on their emotional readiness—the basic ability to build a healthy relationship.

Let's face it. Not everyone has the skills to initiate, build, and sustain good, healthy relationships. Many people grow up in dysfunctional households and never have positive relationships modeled for them. Some people are so focused on themselves and their needs that others might as well not even exist. Still others have been hurt so badly in the past that they see the whole world through the filter of their pain. And because of huge relational blind spots, they don't know themselves or how to relate to people in a healthy way.

It takes relationally healthy people to build great relationships. It all starts there. I believe there are fundamental building blocks that make people ready for relationships. They answer the readiness question. The essential components are contained in the following five People Principles:

The Lens Principle: Who we are determines how we view others.

The Mirror Principle: The first person I must examine is myself.

The Pain Principle: Hurting people hurt people and are easily hurt by them.

The Hammer Principle: Never use a hammer to swat a fly off someone's head.

The Elevator Principle: We can lift people up or take people down in our relationships.

Anyone missing any of these essential components will not be prepared for relationships. And as a result, he will have recurring problems working with others.

If you or someone you know just can't seem to build the kind of positive relationships that all human beings desire, then the reason may be a readiness issue. By learning these five People Principles, you will prepare yourself for the creation of positive, healthy relationships.

THE LENS PRINCIPLE

WHO WE ARE
DETERMINES HOW
WE VIEW OTHERS

*I wouldn't want to belong to any club
that would accept me as a member.*

—GROUCHO MARX

THE QUESTION I MUST ASK MYSELF:
WHAT IS MY PERCEPTION OF OTHERS?

Have you ever started in a new job and had someone with experience in the organization tell you to watch out for this person or steer clear of that person? That's happened to me a number of times. When I took my first professional leadership position, my predecessor told me to watch out for two people: Audrey and Claude. "They'll cause you a lot of problems," I was told. So I went into my job expecting trouble from them.

First, I watched Audrey. She was a strong woman—and she had a strong personality. (It takes one to know one!) To my surprise, working with her ended up being a wonderful experience. She was confident and competent, and she got things done. We had a good working relationship, and she became a family friend. And Claude turned out to be an old farmer who loved the church. True, he was the greatest influencer in the organization. (More than thirty-five years later he still is.) But that didn't hurt my feelings. Why should I have expected a man twice my age who had been in that church all his life to follow me just because I had a leadership position and title? I made it my goal to work with Claude, and he and I got along well.

When I accepted a position at my second church, once again my predecessor warned me: "Watch out for Jim. He'll battle you on everything." So the first week I was there, I met with Jim. We had a difficult conversation, but Jim let me know that he loved God, loved the church, and was with me. He ended up being my number one guy during the years I was there. He went to battle all right—as my strongest supporter. I couldn't have asked for a better team member.

After I had accepted the position at my third church, the leader who preceded me offered to sit down with me and give me a heads-up on those who might cause me problems. As had been the case with the predecessors in the previous two positions, his heart was to help me. But I respectfully declined his offer. By then I'd been in leadership long enough to realize that his problem people wouldn't be mine—and vice versa. I would have no connection with some people he relied on, and others who left him cold would probably become key players for me. Why? Because who we are determines how we view others.

How do you generally perceive the people around you? What has shaped your perception?

_____

_____

_____

You cannot separate your identity from your perspective. All that you are and every experience you've had color how you see things. It is your lens. Here's what I mean:

Who You Are Determines *What You See*

A Coloradan moved to Texas and built a house with a large picture window from which he could view hundreds of miles of rangeland. When asked how he enjoyed the view, he responded, "The only problem is that there's nothing to see." About the same time, a Texan moved to Colorado and built a house with a large picture window overlooking the Rockies. When asked how he liked it, he said, "The only problem with this place is that you can't see anything because all those mountains are in the way."

The story may be a little exaggerated, but it points out a truth just the same. What people see is influenced by who they are. People in the same room will look at the same things and see everything totally differently. That's always true with my wife, Margaret, and me. We'll be at a party chatting with people, and she'll come up and ask, "What was the guy in the blue sweater talking to you about?" I won't have a clue who she means. Margaret has great style and fashion sense. I don't. When I look at people, I don't see what they're wearing. It's all just clothes to me.

Each of us has his or her own bent, and that colors our view of everything. What is around us doesn't determine what we see. What is within us does.

What do you first focus on when introduced to someone new? What kind of details do you notice about a person's appearance or manner?

_____

_____

_____

Who You Are Determines *How You View Others*

A traveler nearing a great city asked an old man seated by the road, "What are the people like in this city?"

"What were they like where you came from?" the man asked.

"Horrible," the traveler reported. "Mean, untrustworthy, detestable in all respects."

"Ah," said the old man, "you will find them the same in the city ahead."

Scarcely had the first traveler gone on his way when another stopped to inquire about the people in the city before him. Again the old man asked about the people in the place the traveler has just left.

"They were fine people: honest, industrious, and generous to a fault," declared the second traveler. "I was sorry to leave."

The old man responded, "That's exactly how you'll find the people here."

The way people view others is a reflection of themselves.

If I am a trusting person, I will view others as trustworthy.

If I am a critical person, I will view others as critical.

If I am a caring person, I will view others as compassionate.

Your personality comes through when you talk about others and interact with them. Someone who doesn't know you would be able to tell a lot about who you are based on simple observation.

How would you describe the people you work with or see regularly?

_____

_____

Examine your statement. What did you focus on (strengths, weaknesses, skills, personality, etc.)? What do your comments reveal about your personality and experience?

_____

_____

_____

Who You Are Determines *How You View Life*

We all have a personal frame of reference that consists of our attitudes, assumptions, and expectations concerning ourselves, other people, and life. These factors determine whether we're optimistic or pessimistic, cheerful or gloomy, trusting or suspicious, friendly or reserved, brave or timid. And they color not only how we see life, but also how we let people treat us. Eleanor Roosevelt said, "No one can make you feel inferior without your consent." Or to put it another way, in the words of psychologist and author Phil McGraw, "You teach people how to treat you." What you teach comes from how you see life. And how you see life comes from who you are.

A few years ago, I had the opportunity to teach leadership to the NFL's St. Louis Rams. The team invited me to attend one of their games afterward, and I was allowed to sit with the spouses of the coaches and players. I sat next to Kim Matsko, wife of associate head coach/offensive line coach of the St. Louis Rams, John Matsko. As we chatted, I asked her of all the cities where she had lived, what was her favorite? (She had lived in many states: Ohio, North Carolina, Arizona, California, New York, and Missouri.) Her response, "Where I am living right now."

"Oh, so you like St. Louis the best?" I said.

"No, I didn't say that. I like the place I'm currently living best," she answered. "It's a choice." What a great attitude! If you can maintain a perspective like that, you will always view life in a positive light.

Have you ever chosen to be content with your current location or situation? What unsettled area of your life can you choose right now to view with a more positive attitude? How do you think this positive choice will affect your interaction with others?

_____

_____

_____

Who You Are Determines *What You Do*

It's easy to see that natural ability affects what we do. But our thinking and our attitude are as much parts of us as our talents and abilities. They also determine what we do. We cannot separate them, and if we expect results different from our makeup, we're in for disappointment.

FIVE THINGS THAT DETERMINE WHO WE ARE

What factors come into play in determining who you are? Maybe you've never given this much thought. Obviously there are many, but here are what I consider to be the top five. For each area listed, give an example of how it has influenced the person you are today.

1. Genetics

_____
_____
_____

2. Self-Image

_____
_____
_____

3. Experiences in Life

_____
_____
_____

4. Attitude and Choices about Those Experiences

_____
_____
_____

5. Friends

_____
_____
_____

APPLYING THE LENS PRINCIPLE

1. Would you describe your attitude as generally positive or negative? (Don't cop out and call yourself a realist. Which way do you lean?) Do you see your attitude as an asset or a liability? What could you do to improve your attitude?

_____
_____

2. Think back to your childhood. What experiences have especially marked you as an individual? Did they inspire you to trust or mistrust people? How has that outlook colored your relationships as an adult? If it has negatively affected your relationships, what positive experiences can you pursue to create a new, more positive history?

_____

_____

_____

3. Do you agree with the statement that the difference between who you are today and who you will be in five years will be the people you spend time with and the books you read? What other factors do you believe to be equally (or more) important?

_____

_____

_____

4. Think about the personal qualities you would like to cultivate. List them. Now, create a plan for growth to develop those qualities. First, dedicate time on your calendar with people who possess the qualities you desire. Second, select a book a month to read to help you grow.

_____

_____

_____

Summary

The way you view others is determined by who you are. You cannot get away from that truth. If you don't like people, it really is a statement about you, since who you are determines how you view others. Your viewpoint is the problem. If that's the case, don't try to change others. Don't even focus on others; focus on yourself. If you change yourself and become the kind of person you desire to be, you will begin to view others in a whole new light. And that will change the way you interact in all of your relationships.

THE MIRROR PRINCIPLE

THE FIRST PERSON
WE MUST EXAMINE
IS OURSELVES

Coping with difficult people is always a problem,
especially if the difficult person happens to be you.

THE QUESTION I MUST ASK MYSELF:
HAVE I EXAMINED MYSELF AND
TAKEN RESPONSIBILITY FOR WHO I AM?

Have you ever known someone who was his own worst enemy, who always managed to short-circuit himself when success was within reach, or who could not seem to hold down a job? Some of these people possess great potential but keep blowing themselves up. But not everyone with these kinds of issues is a person who can't get ahead in life. Sometimes people who are their own worst enemies achieve big things while slowly chipping away at themselves and their relationships with others. I believe Pete Rose is one such person.

A ROSE BY ANY OTHER NAME

When it comes to playing baseball, few people compare to Pete Rose. Here are just a few of his major-league baseball records:

- Most career hits (4,256)
- Most games played (3,562)
- Most at bats (14,053)
- Most total bases by a switch-hitter (5,752)
- Most seasons of 200 or more hits (10)
- Most seasons with 600 or more at bats (17)
- National League record for most career runs (2,165)
- National League record for most years played (24)[1]

Rose, who was a Gold Glove outfielder for two seasons, also has received numerous awards: he was named the National League Rookie of the Year (1963), the National League Most Valuable Player (1973), and the World Series MVP (1975).[2]

But while Pete Rose was succeeding on the baseball field, he was failing in other areas of his life. Specifically the thing that was causing chaos in his personal life and that would eventually end his baseball career was gambling.

Ever since the World Series betting scandal in the early 1900s, major-league baseball has worked to keep gambling out of the sport. In every major-league baseball clubhouse in the United States, Rule 21(d) is posted where players and coaches can see it. The rule states,

Any player, umpire, or club or league official or employee, who shall bet any sum whatsoever upon any baseball game in connection with which the bettor has no duty to perform, shall be declared ineligible for one year.

Any player, umpire, or club or league official or employee, who shall bet any sum whatsoever upon any baseball game in connection with which the bettor has a duty to perform shall be declared permanently ineligible.[3]

Pete Rose must have walked past that posted rule at least 3,562 games as a player, because that's how many games he played in. He saw it at least an additional 554 times as a manager.[4] Yet he still bet on baseball. And in January 2004, after denying it for fourteen years, Rose finally admitted to betting on baseball, including making bets on his own team, the Cincinnati Reds.

BLIND SPOT

When Pete Rose began betting on baseball in 1987, he said he "didn't even consider the consequences."[5] Perhaps it was just a natural next step in his progression as a compulsive gambler—a label that Rose vehemently says does not describe him.[6] But what else would you call a person who bet year-round on football, basketball, and baseball, who could not stop gambling even when it might cost him his livelihood, and who spent mind-boggling sums on bets? Bookmaker Ron Peters testified that he took more than $1 million in bets from Rose. Just on baseball. Just in one season![7]

How could Rose not see what was happening to him? Why didn't he keep himself from gambling on baseball? How could he continue to lie about what he'd done for more than a decade? How could he say that his only real problem was the friends he picked? How could he continue to say that he didn't have a problem? I believe the answer is that he was focused so intently on baseball that he never really looked in the mirror and examined himself.

TAKE A GOOD LOOK

Rose realized he was different from other players, but he rarely stopped to reflect on whether that was a positive or a negative thing. He says, "Joe Morgan [Rose's former teammate who is now in the Hall of Fame] used to say that he felt sorry for me because when baseball was all over, I would have nothing else in my life to occupy my time. I never understood Joe's way of thinking. I always thought he was somehow less committed than me, that he didn't love the game as much as I did. Who in his right mind could ever put anything in life ahead of baseball?"[8]

While Rose was playing, his refusal to examine himself didn't hurt his career, although it did damage his personal relationships. But once his playing days were over, it caught up with him. Rose states,

> In hindsight I should have taken some time to reflect on my life, on where I'd been and where I was headed. If I had been a book reader, I could have read up on how other famous folks handled retirement . . . I could have called Dick Butkus and asked how he felt about retiring from the NFL after achieving godlike status as a player. I could have called Terry Bradshaw . . . But I didn't find out how any of them dealt with retirement because I never talked to them. I never talked to anybody. It wasn't my style.[9]

In one of his rare moments of reflection and genuine self-assessment, Rose sums up the way he handled himself: "I was aware of my records and my place in baseball history. But I was never aware of boundaries or able to control that part of my life. And admitting that I was out of control has been next to impossible for me. I was aware of my privileges, but not my responsibilities."[10] In my opinion, he's still struggling to figure out what his responsibilities are. That's very hard to do when you don't like looking in the mirror.

THE MIRROR TEST

People unaware of who they are and what they do often damage their relationships with others. The way to change that is to look in the mirror. It's something all of us must do. It's what I call taking the mirror test. Consider these truths that we must learn about ourselves:

The First Person I Must Know Is Myself—Self-Awareness

Human nature seems to endow people with the ability to size up everybody in the world but themselves. Pete Rose does not have a clear image of himself. He tends to think of himself as a victim. Rose has described himself as a kid from the wrong side of the tracks and as someone who got by with only average athletic talent. And he thinks that the punishment he has received (being banned from baseball) does not fit his crime.[11]

Some people are endowed with natural self-awareness. Thomas Armstrong, author of *7 Kinds of Smart*, points out that these kinds of people possess intrapersonal intelligence. However, becoming self-aware does not come easily for most people. It is a process—sometimes a slow one—that requires intentionality.

Ask a trusted friend to write out a short description of your strengths, your weaknesses, what makes you unique, what they think your priorities are, and the impression you give people who don't know you as well as they do. Ask him or her to describe how you react when things are going great and when things are disappointing or stressful. Take time to write out your own description of yourself, and then compare the two lists. Where were you on target? What surprised you?

_____

_____

_____

What are some common misconceptions people have about you? Why do you think they have these misconceptions? How can you change your behavior to more accurately represent your true self?

_____

_____

_____

The First Person I Must Get Along with Is Myself—Self-Image

Author Sydney J. Harris observed, "If you're not comfortable with yourself you can't be comfortable with others." I would take that one step farther. If you do not believe in yourself, you will sabotage relationships.

When it comes to relationships, self-image is the relational lid. Your image of yourself restricts your ability to build healthy relationships. A negative self-image will even keep a person from being successful. And even when a person with a poor self-image does somehow achieve success, it won't last because he will eventually bring himself down to the level of his own expectations. In a backward sort of way, it's a tribute to Pete Rose's self-confidence that his lack of self-awareness didn't catch up with him sooner.

Most people carry around a mental list of what they don't like about themselves. Now it's time to write out all the things you do like about yourself. Try this week to concentrate on the outstanding qualities you possess that can contribute to those around you.

\
\
\

The First Person to Cause Me Problems Is Myself—Self-Honesty

Comedian Jack Parr quipped, "Looking back, my life seems like one big obstacle race, with me being the chief obstacle." He was making a joke, but what he says is still true for most of us. Pete Rose isn't alone in his ability to cause problems for himself. That's an issue for me. And it is for you, too. If we could kick the person responsible for most of our troubles, we wouldn't be able to sit down for weeks. What can save us is the willingness to look in the mirror and get honest about our shortcomings, faults, and problems.

Think about the last few obstacles you've encountered. How did you contribute to the problems? What did you do that helped bring about solutions?

\
\
\

The First Person I Must Change Is Myself—Self-Improvement

A danger of teaching conferences or writing is that people start to assume you're an expert who has mastered everything you teach. Don't believe it. Like you, I'm still working on my relational and leadership skills. There are principles in this workbook that I don't do well, so I'm still working to improve myself. And that will always be true for me. If I ever think I've finished growing, then I'm in trouble.

What are you doing or what can you do to improve yourself this month?

_____

_____

_____

The First Person who Can Make a Difference Is Myself—Self-Responsibility

In *The 17 Indisputable Laws of Teamwork,* I wrote about the Law of Significance: "One is too small a number to achieve greatness." I truly believe that no significant accomplishments can be achieved by individual effort. However, I also believe that every significant accomplishment begins with the vision of one individual. That person not only possesses the vision but also takes responsibility for carrying it to others. If you want to make a difference in this world, you must take responsibility for yourself.

APPLYING THE MIRROR PRINCIPLE

1. If you were to ask family members, friends, and colleagues which of your practices and habits are causing you more harm than good, what would they say? (If you have the courage, really ask them this question.) How do those factors affect your relationships?

_____

_____

_____

2. Where does personal reflection fit into the Mirror Principle? How likely are people in our culture to set aside time for self-examination? Explain your answer. When, where, how long, and how often do you examine your character, review your habits, and critique your practices? How can you improve in this area?

_____

_____

_____

3. How would you describe yourself? Overall, have you experienced more wins or losses in life? What do you expect the future to hold? How has your past colored your perspective?

_____

_____

_____

4. One of the knocks against the current "self-worth" movement is that it encourages people to think highly of themselves regardless of character or performance. Why is it important to be sure self-image is grounded in truth? How can one guard against false pride and still have confidence in himself?

_____

_____

_____

5. In what area do you need the greatest growth? How have you taken responsibility for it? What is your plan to improve in this area? Have you dedicated resources to it and put it on your calendar? If not, why not? How can you improve in this area?

_____

_____

_____

Summary

Psychotherapist Sheldon Kopp believes "all the significant battles are waged within the self." As we examine ourselves, we discover what those battles are. And then we have two choices. The first is to be like the man who visited his doctor and found out he had serious health issues. When the doctor showed him his X-rays and suggested a painful and expensive surgery, the man asked, "Okay, but how much would you charge to just touch up the X-rays?"

The second choice is to stop blaming others, look at ourselves, and do the hard work of resolving the issues that are causing us problems. If you want to have better relationships with others, then stop, look in the mirror, and start working on yourself.

THE PAIN PRINCIPLE

HURTING PEOPLE HURT PEOPLE AND ARE EASILY HURT BY THEM

*"Be yourself" is
about the worst advice you
can give some people!*

THE QUESTION I MUST ASK MYSELF:
DO I HURT PEOPLE,
OR AM I TOO EASILY HURT BY THEM?

I n 1972, I accepted an invitation to lead my second church. It was a wonderful opportunity since the church was larger and more established than my previous one. And it was in a nice town, Lancaster, Ohio. It was an exciting time for Margaret and me.

MY NEW PEN PAL

I had been at the church only ten days when I received a piece of mail from Rick, a member of the congregation. I opened it up, began reading, and soon discovered that it was a typed transcript of the sermon I had delivered on my first Sunday. I was amazed—and flattered—that someone had taken the time to capture every word I had said. And then I looked more carefully. The pages were covered with comments. Rick had red-penned every grammatical mistake, corrected every misspoken word, and pointed out any factual error.

I thought it was odd, but I didn't worry too much about it. I know I'm not perfect, and I'm aware that I sometimes make mistakes when I speak. But I have a healthy self-image, so I didn't let it bother me. But then the next week, another envelope arrived in the mail from Rick. Once again, the message I had preached the previous Sunday had been transcribed. And once again, every tiny mistake was marked in red ink. That's when I figured I'd better meet Rick and find out what was bothering him.

The next Sunday after delivering the message, I asked someone to point out Rick to me. I walked over to him, stuck out my hand, and said, "Hi, I'm John Maxwell."

At first Rick just stared at me. Finally he said, "Hello, *Pastor*." And that's when I realized he wasn't going to shake my hand. Then he turned on his heel and walked away.

Sure enough, a couple of days later, guess what I received in the mail? Another envelope from Rick. I started calling them his love letters. I got one every week with his in-depth critique. Would you care to guess how long I received Rick's love letters? Seven years! During that time, he never voluntarily shook my hand. I tried to connect with him, but he wanted little to do with me. In only one subject could I get him to engage in conversation with me. Our kids were adopted and so were his, so he'd talk to me about them. But he wouldn't warm up.

WHAT LIES BENEATH

Then one day I had lunch with a veteran pastor. I told him about Rick, the weekly love letters I received, and my inability to win Rick over. My pastor friend looked at me and said, "You know, John, hurting people hurt people." That statement really connected for me. "Whenever someone says or does something hurtful," he continued, "you need to go beneath the surface."

I looked at Rick in a new way after that. I began searching for the cause of his pain, and I tried again to connect with him. Finally one day when I was trying to get him to engage, he made a statement that more than hinted at the problem. He said, "Never trust a pastor." I later came to find out that Rick had once served as a board member at a church and had been mistreated by the pastor. He decided from then on that pastors were bad news and couldn't be trusted.

After I understood the problem, I was able to work on winning Rick's trust. It took a lot of effort, but by the time I left Lancaster to accept another leadership position, Rick had gotten over his mistrust of me. We became friends. And not only was he willing to shake my hand, but he'd give me a great big bear hug. By then, he had long since given up sending me love letters.

SOME PAIN, NO GAIN

To really understand the Pain Principle and have it help you in dealing with others, you need to keep in mind four truths:

1. There Are Many Hurting People

Of course, the fact that many people are hurting is not a new phenomenon. Columnist Ann Landers asserted that one in four Americans is imbalanced. (She added that we should look at our three closest friends, and if they seem okay, it means we're the one!) We can't be naive about the hurts of people, but I believe there is hope for everyone.

Who do you know personally that is hurting? What is causing their pain?

_____

_____

_____

2. Those Hurting People Often Hurt People

German poet Herman Hesse wrote, "If you hate a person, you hate something in him that is part of yourself. What isn't part of ourselves doesn't disturb us." I agree with his viewpoint. When hurting people lash out, it is in response to what's happening inside them more than what's happening around them. They feel or believe something negative within themselves. The problem is that people who don't believe in themselves will never succeed, and they will also keep those around them from succeeding.

Think about the last time you hurt someone. Describe the situation. Based on Hesse's statement, what was happening in you that resulted in your actions?

_____

_____

_____

3. Those Hurting People Are Often Hurt by People

Not only do hurting people hurt others, but they are also easily hurt by others. My friend Kevin Myers illustrates it this way. If someone has a splinter in his finger and he allows it to remain there, his finger becomes swollen and infected. Then if another person barely brushes against it, the individual howls with pain and says, "You hurt me!" But the reality is that the problem isn't with the person who innocently bumped the finger. It's with the person who has the splinter but has neglected to address the injury.

Emotional pain works in a similar way. Hurting people overreact, overexaggerate, and overprotect. As you interact with others, remember this: anytime a person's response is larger than the issue at hand, the response is almost always about something else.

Describe a situation where someone overacted. What do you think was at the core of this person's reaction?

_____

_____

_____

4. Those Hurting People Often Hurt Themselves

In an old comedy routine, a know-it-all is fond of lecturing his friend at the station where they wait to take the commuter train each morning. And every time the know-it-all talks, he pokes his friend in the chest with his finger. That, of course, doesn't sit well with the other man. So he finally determines that he's going to put a stop to it.

The next day on the way to the station, he meets a third friend and says, "I'm so tired of that know-it-all lecturing me and poking me in the chest. Today I'm going to get 'im."

"How are you going to do that?" his buddy asks.

The first man opens his coat to reveal three sticks of dynamite strapped to his chest. "Today when he pokes me," he says with a smile, "he's going to blow his hand off."

Hurting people are often like that. They may hurt others, but the ones they hurt deepest and most often are themselves. Poet George Herbert declared, "He who cannot forgive others breaks the bridge over which he must pass himself."

DEALING WITH HURTING PEOPLE

Author Glenn Clark advises, "If you wish to travel far and fast, travel light. Take off all your envies, jealousies, unforgiveness, selfishness, and tears." People who have not gotten past their hurt have a hard time doing that. As a result, they act and react differently from healthy people.

HEALTHY PEOPLE ARE . . .	HURTING PEOPLE ARE . . .
More willing to change.	Less willing to change.
More willing to admit failure.	Less willing to admit failure.
More willing to discuss issues.	Less willing to discuss issues.
More willing to learn from others.	Less willing to learn from others.
More willing to do something about the problem.	Less willing to do something about the problem.
Able to travel light.	Carrying a lot of baggage.

If you find yourself dealing with a hurting person, which we all must do from time to time, then I advise that you do the following:

Don't Take It Personally

Hurting people are going to find offense when none is given. When you know that you've done nothing wrong, remember that it's not what others say about you; it's what you believe about yourself. You can apologize for their pain and feel compassion for their state, but you should try not to take it personally. That can be difficult—even for a person with a healthy self-image—but it's worth the effort.

Look Beyond the Person for the Problem

Just as I did with Rick, you would do well to try to look past the person and his hurtful actions and try to see what's causing him pain. Even if you can't discover the source of the problem, this plan will help you to approach the person with greater compassion.

Look Beyond the Situation

Have you ever had to make a bad-news phone call and dreaded it, not so much because of the news you have to deliver but because you're dreading the response from the person on the other end of the line? Just last week, Margaret and I had to make such a call. The weekend had been planned, but at the last minute things changed. We had to call a friend who would be negatively affected by the change. We hated to make the call, not because the news was that bad, but because the person is not always emotionally strong and would react badly.

In such cases, try not to focus on the situation. Just remember that it's not what happens to you; it's what happens in you that matters. Try to rise above the emotional turmoil that the other person may create.

Do Not Add to Their Hurt

The natural inclination for many people is to meet fire with fire, pain with pain. But striking back at a hurting person is like kicking a man while he's down. Statesman Sir Francis Bacon said, "This is certain, that a man that studieth revenge keeps his wounds green, which otherwise would heal and do well." If someone lashes out at you, the best thing to do is to forgive him and move on.

Help Them Find Help

The kindest thing you can do for hurting people is to try to get them help. Some people don't want to deal with their issues, and you certainly can't force them to receive help. But you can always choose to extend your hand. It may take a long time, as it did with Rick, but even very bitter people have been known to come around.

WHAT IF YOU'RE THE ONE WHO'S HURTING?

At the beginning of this chapter, the question was asked: *Do I hurt people, or am I too easily hurt by them?* If you answered yes, then you need to answer a second question: *Am I prepared to work through my issues and get beyond my pain?* Here's the key. Most people just want a quick fix, something to give them some relief in the moment. That's why some choose to lash out; it makes them feel better in the moment. Others use alcohol, food, sex, or something else to lessen the pain. But as my friend Kevin Myers says, "If you want to become well, you need more than a fix. You need to become fit."

People who seek emotional fitness don't look for momentary relief. They search for what's right. How can you tell what kind of person you are? People searching for a fix stop working at fixing a problem as soon as the pain or pressure is relieved. People seeking fitness continue doing what's right and improving themselves even when the discomfort goes away.

Delving into your old hurts and emotional issues often takes the help of a professional counselor and can be a messy proposition, but it's worth it. If your relational capacity is all "clogged up," you may have to do some digging to make things right. And you may have to deal with some pretty nasty stuff. But the reward is that you may discover some treasures that you didn't know existed. And at the end of your hard work, you can develop a healthy capacity for relationships.

APPLYING THE PAIN PRINCIPLE

1. Do you agree that we are most likely to react negatively to something in another person that we dislike about ourselves? Explain.

_____

_____

_____

2. Do you find it difficult to separate the person or situation from the pain he causes? Explain. What strategies can one use to do that effectively?

_____

_____

_____

3. In general, are you more likely to be someone who unintentionally hurts others or who is hurt by others who are hurting? Explain.

_____

_____

_____

4. How do you maintain compassion for hurting people without encouraging them to wallow in their pain or dumping on you? Where can a hurting person get help? Explain ways you might assist a hurting person to get help that are sensitive yet effective.

_____

_____

_____

Summary

When someone is hurt by something you say or do, the best thing you can do is apologize quickly and sincerely. But when others overreact to something you do—and you've examined yourself honestly to be sure the reaction outweighs the offense—then remember that the person is hurting. Be kind and gentle. And don't take their reaction personally.

THE HAMMER PRINCIPLE

Never Use a Hammer to Swat a Fly Off Someone's Head

If you would win the world,
melt it, do not hammer it.

—Alexander MacLaren

THE QUESTION I MUST ASK MYSELF:
WOULD OTHERS SAY I OVERREACT
TO SMALL THINGS IN A RELATIONSHIP?

My wife, Margaret, and I were married in June 1969, and like most couples, we naively believed that nothing but smooth sailing lay ahead of us. Of course, it didn't take long for us to find ourselves in the kinds of minor disagreements that all couples experience, especially when they're first adjusting to married life.

Like most people, I thought I was right nearly all of the time, and I let Margaret know about it. I've always been a good talker, and I can be pretty persuasive, so I used my skills to win our arguments. We never yelled or screamed at each other. It was always very rational and controlled, but I always made sure I won. The problem was that with my approach, Margaret always had to lose.

We did a lot of things right during those first two years of marriage, but this wasn't one of them. Unknowingly I was slowly but surely beating Margaret down emotionally. We'd disagree, I'd overreact, and I'd unwittingly lay another brick in the wall that was building between us. I didn't realize that winning at all costs could eventually jeopardize our marriage. Then one day Margaret sat me down, shared how she felt when we argued, and explained what it was doing to our relationship. It was the first time I understood I was putting winning the arguments ahead of winning the relationship.

From that day I decided to change. Realizing that having the right attitude was more important than having the right answers, I softened my approach, listened more, and stopped making a big deal out of little things. In time, the wall that had begun to form came down, and we began building bridges. And since that time, I've made a conscious effort to initiate connection anytime I'm in conflict with someone I care about.

IF I HAD A HAMMER . . .

Let's face it. Because of their personalities, some people are inclined to use a hammer, even when something gentler will do. I must admit I find myself on the verge of overreaction more times than I'd like. So when tempted to use overkill, I try to temper my behavior using the following four Ts. You may want to embrace them when you find yourself in a similar situation.

1. Total Picture

Do you come to conclusions long before the problem has been laid out before you? That is a common occurrence for most of us who have strong personalities. That's why I have trained myself to follow a process to keep me from hammering people with answers before they've finished asking the question. When someone is sharing his point of view with me, I try to . . .

listen,
ask questions,
listen again,
ask more questions,
listen some more,
then
respond.

I find that if I slow myself down, I am likely to respond more patiently and appropriately.

Why is it beneficial to have the total picture before responding?

_____

_____

_____

2. Timing

When you act is as important as taking the right action. If you don't apologize to someone when you've wronged him, the relationship might be lost. And knowing when not to act can be just as important. Noted hostess and writer Lady Dorothy Nevill observed, "The real art of conversation is not only to say the right thing in the right place, but to leave unsaid the wrong thing at the tempting moment."

It seems to me that the most common cause of bad timing in relationships is selfish motives. (If you have small children, think about their timing. It's often poor, but that's because they usually think only of themselves.) For that reason, when little things bother us, our number one objective must be putting our personal agendas aside and building the relationship.

If you have examined your motives, and you can be certain they're good, then you need to ask yourself two timing questions. First, *am I ready to confront?* That's a pretty easy question to answer, because that's really a matter of whether you've done your homework. The second is harder: *Is the other person ready to hear?* If you've laid a relational foundation and the two of you are not in the "heat of battle," then the answer may be yes.

3. Tone

People often respond to our attitudes and actions more than to our words. Many petty conflicts occur because people use the wrong tone of voice. The writer of Proverbs stated, "A soft answer turns away wrath, but a harsh word stirs up anger."[1] Haven't you found that to be true? If not, try this experiment. The next time someone says something to you in anger, respond with gentleness and kindness. When you do that, the person who spoke harshly is likely to tone down, if not soften, his attitude.

4. Temperature

As tempers flare, people are prone to dropping bombs when using a slingshot will do. And that can cause a lot of trouble because the size of a problem often changes based on how it is handled. In general . . .

> If the reaction is worse than the action, the problem usually increases.
> If the reaction is less than the action, the problem usually decreases.

That's why I try to follow a self-imposed guideline that I call the Reprimand Rule: "Take thirty seconds to share feelings—and then it's over." Anytime we let a little thing create a big reaction (one that lasts longer than thirty seconds), then we're using a hammer.

Do you often find yourself in a heated discussion where you don't remember what started the argument? If so, why? How could the Reprimand Rule help you?

_____

_____

_____

TRADE IN YOUR HAMMER FOR A VELVET GLOVE

Some people seem to think that a hammer is good for anything and everything. I guess you could say they take a hammering approach to life. I've observed this attitude most often among high achievers. When they give something their attention, they go at it full bore. That's usually a good approach to tasks. It's a terrible way to treat people, however. As psychologist Abraham Maslow observed, "If the only tool you have is a hammer, you tend to see every problem as a nail." People require more judicious treatment than that.

If you desire to develop a softer touch with people, take the following advice to heart:

Let the Past Stay in the Past

Resolve an issue when it occurs. And once you've done that, don't bring it up again. If you do, you're treating someone as a nail.

Ask Yourself, *Is My Reaction Part of the Problem?*

As I mentioned in the Pain Principle, when a person's response is greater than the issue, the response is about something else. Don't make things worse by overreacting.

Remember that Actions Are Remembered Long After Words Are Forgotten

If you have a high school diploma or college degree, can you recall the message the commencement speaker delivered at your graduation? Or if you're married, can you recite your wedding vows from memory? I'm guessing the answer to both questions is no. But I bet you do remember getting married and receiving your diploma. The way you *treat* people will stay with them a lot longer than the words you choose. Act accordingly.

Do you agree that actions are remembered longer than words?
Give an example.

_____

_____

_____

Never Let the Situation Mean More than the Relationship

I believe that if I hadn't made my relationship with Margaret a higher priority than always being right, we might not be married today. Relationships are based on bonding. The more important the relationship, the greater the bond. There will be more about this in the Situation Principle.

Think about your strongest relationships. How have you managed to disagree without damaging the relationship? (If you have damaged the relationships, think about what drives you to put your opinions ahead of the person.)

_____

_____

_____

Treat Loved Ones with Unconditional Love

Because ours is a society with lots of broken and dysfunctional individuals, many people have never had good models of unconditional love. In *The Flight*, John Whit gave his perspective on where we fall short in our treatment of the important people in our lives: "We gossip because we fail to love. When we love people, we don't criticize them. If we love them, their failures hurt. We don't advertise the sins of people we love any more than we advertise our own."

Admit Wrongs and Ask Forgiveness

Admitting you're wrong and asking for forgiveness covers a multitude of sins. That approach is also one of the best ways to try to make things right when you find that you've used the hammer instead of the velvet glove.

APPLYING THE HAMMER PRINCIPLE

1. In what situations are you most tempted to use the hammer instead of the velvet glove? Why is that? How can you anticipate when that is about to happen and change it?

_____

_____

_____

2. Some people are naturally inclined to look at the total picture; others are prone to focus on details. Which are you? What can you do to improve your ability to see things in context and make you less likely to jump to conclusions?

_____

_____

_____

3. Think of someone who is a master at using the velvet glove. What makes him or her so good with people? What can you learn from this individual?

_____

_____

_____

4. How would you define *unconditional love*? What gets in the way of loving others unconditionally? How can one love others unconditionally and still maintain high personal and professional standards?

_____

_____

_____

5. What happens inside you when another person admits wrongdoing and apologizes? How does that affect the relationship in the future? If it has such a positive effect, then why are we so reluctant to do it? How can we get over that reluctance?

_____

_____

_____

Summary

The problem with most individuals who use the hammer all the time is that they may not know they do it. A recent article by executive coach Marshall Goldsmith told about a man named Mike who was a top-performing investment banker. Goldsmith was asked to help him because he was a hammer wielder. Mike saw himself as "a warrior on Wall Street but a pussycat at home." Goldsmith instructed Mike to call his wife to confirm his self-assessment, and much to his surprise, she said that he was a jerk at home, too. When his children confirmed her assessment, Mike finally began to see himself as others did.

Goldsmith's advice is this: "Let your colleagues hold the mirror and tell you what they see. If you don't believe them, do the same with your loved ones and friends."[2] If you do that, you will find out whether you treat others as people or as nails. If you do the latter, then you need to make a change.

THE ELEVATOR PRINCIPLE

WE CAN LIFT PEOPLE UP
OR TAKE PEOPLE DOWN
IN OUR RELATIONSHIPS

People can be the wind beneath our wings
or the anchor on our boat.

> THE QUESTION I MUST ASK MYSELF:
> WOULD OTHERS SAY THAT I LIFT THEM UP
> OR TAKE THEM DOWN?

I n the 1920s, physician, consultant, and psychologist George W. Crane began teaching
social psychology at Northwestern University in Chicago. Though he was new to
teaching, he was an astute student of human nature, and he believed strongly in making the study of psychology practical to his students.

One of the first classes he taught contained evening students who were older than the
average college student. The young men and women worked in the department stores,
offices, and factories of Chicago by day and were trying to improve themselves by attend-
ing classes at night.

After class one evening a young woman named Lois, who had moved to Chicago from
a small town in Wisconsin to take a civil service job, confided in Crane that she felt isolated and lonely. "I don't know anybody, except a few girls at the office," she lamented.
"At night I go to my room and write letters home. The only thing that keeps me living
from day to day is the hope of receiving a letter from my friends in Wisconsin."

A NEW KIND OF CLUB

It was largely in response to Lois's problem that Crane came up with what he called the
Compliment Club, which he announced to his class the following week. It was to be the
first of several practical assignments he would give them that term.

"You are to use your psychology every day either at home or at work or on the street-
cars and buses," Crane told them. "For the first month, your written assignment will be
the *Compliment Club*. Every day you are to pay an honest compliment to each of three
different persons. You can increase that number if you wish, but to qualify for a class
grade, you must have complimented at least three people every day for thirty days . . .

"Then, at the end of the thirty-day experiment, I want you to write a theme or paper
on your experiences," he continued. "Include the changes you have noted in the people
around you, as well as your own altered outlook on life."[1]

Some of Crane's students resisted this assignment. Some complained that they wouldn't
know what to say. Others were afraid of being rejected. And a few thought it would be

dishonest to compliment someone they didn't like. "Suppose you meet somebody you dislike?" one man asked. "Wouldn't it be insincere to praise your enemy?"

"No, it is not insincerity when you compliment your enemy," Crane responded, "for the compliment is an honest statement of praise for some objective trait or merit that deserves commendation. You will find that nobody is entirely devoid of merit or virtue . . . Your praise may buoy up the morale of lonely souls who are almost ready to give up the struggle to do good deeds. You never know when your casual compliment may catch a boy or girl, or man or woman, at the critical point when he would otherwise toss in the sponge."[2]

Crane's students discovered that their sincere compliments had a positive impact on the people around them. And the experience made an even greater impact on the students themselves. Lois blossomed into a real people person who lit up a room when she entered it. And another student, who was ready to quit her job as a legal secretary because of an especially difficult boss, began complimenting him, even though at first she did so through clenched teeth. Eventually not only did his surliness toward her change, but so did her exasperation with him. They wound up taking a genuine liking to each other and were married.

George Crane's Compliment Club probably sounds a little bit corny to us today. But the principles behind it are just as sound now as they were in the 1920s. The bottom line is that Crane was teaching what I call the Elevator Principle: we can lift people up or take people down in our relationships. He was trying to teach his students to be proactive. Crane said, "The world is starving for appreciation. It is hungry for compliments. But somebody must start the ball rolling by speaking first and saying a nice thing to his companion."[3] He embraced the sentiment of Benjamin Franklin, who believed, "As we must account for every idle word—so we must for every idle silence."

Who have you complimented this week and how did you do it?

_____

_____

_____

WHAT KIND OF PERSON ARE YOU?

Are you the type of person to lift others up, or do you tend to lean on others? Are you easing someone's load or are you asking someone else to take on your responsibilities?

These are good questions we must ask ourselves because our answers will have a huge impact on our relationships. People tend to add value to others, lessening their load and lifting them up, or they take away value from others, thinking only of themselves and taking people down in the process. But I would take that one step farther. I believe the intensity with which we lift or lower others can determine the *four* kinds of people there are when it comes to relationships:

1. Some People *Add* Something to Life—We Enjoy Them

Many people in this world desire to help others. These people are adders. They make the lives of others more pleasant and enjoyable. People who add value to others almost always do so *intentionally*. I say that because adding value to others requires a person to give of himself, and that rarely occurs by accident.

Years ago, my nephew, Troy, came to live with Margaret and me after he finished college and went to work at a mortgage company. Troy was smart, he was a hard worker, and he wanted to be successful. And we wanted to help him. So I gave him some advice as we went off to his new job. I suggested that he do these things:

- *Go early and stay late—do more than is expected.* I advised him to arrive at work thirty minutes early, eat lunch in half the time allotted, and work thirty minutes after quitting time.

- *Do something every day to help the people around him.* I suggested that he add value to the team by adding value to his coworkers.

- *Offer to go the extra mile for the boss.* I told him to make an appointment with his boss and let him know that if he needed anything extra done—no matter how menial—he was available to help. And that meant after hours or on the weekend.

What I was doing was giving Troy a lesson in becoming an adder. And Troy added value to the people around him and to the company—so much so that he was promoted very quickly and was rising high in the organization before his 30th birthday.

How do you (or how will you) exceed the expectations of those around you?

_____

_____

_____

2. Some People Subtract Something from Life—We Tolerate Them

In *Julius Caesar*, playwright William Shakespeare's Cassius asserts, "A friend should bear his friend's infirmities, / But Brutus makes mine greater than they are." That's what subtracters do. They do not bear our burdens, and they make heavier the ones we already have. The sad thing about subtracters is that what they do is usually unintentional. If you don't know how to add to others, then you probably subtract by default.

Who are the subtracters in your life? How do you feel when you are around them?

_____

_____

_____

3. Some People *Multiply* Something in Life—We Value Them

Anyone who wants to can become an adder. It takes only a desire to lift people up and the intentionality to follow through. That is what George Crane was trying to teach his students. But to go to another level in relationships—to become a multiplier—one must be intentional, strategic, and skilled. The greater the talent and resources a person possesses, the greater his potential to become a multiplier.

Who are the multipliers in your life? How have they risen beyond being adders?

_____

_____

_____

4. Some People Divide Something in Life—We Avoid Them

Dividers are people who will really "take you to the basement," meaning they'll take you down as low as they can, as often as they can. They're like the company president who sent his personnel director a memo, saying, "Search the organization for an alert, aggressive young man who could step into my shoes—and when you find him, fire him."

Dividers are so damaging because unlike subtracters, their negative actions are usually intentional. They are hurtful people who make themselves look or feel better by trying to make someone else do worse than they do. As a result, they damage relationships and create havoc in people's lives.

Do you know someone who fits the description of a divider? How can you limit your time with this person?

_____

_____

_____

TAKE OTHERS TO A HIGHER LEVEL

I believe that deep down everyone—even the most negative person—wants to be a lifter. We all want to be a positive influence in the lives of others. And we can be. If you want to lift people up and add value to their lives, keep the following in mind:

Lifters Commit Themselves to Daily Encouragement

Roman philosopher Lucius Annaeus Seneca observed, "Wherever there is a human being, there is an opportunity for kindness." If you want to lift people up, take George Crane's advice. Encourage others and do it daily.

Lifters Know the Little Difference that Separates Hurting and Helping

The little things you do every day have a greater impact on others than you might think. You hold the power to make another person's life better or worse by the things you do today. Those closest to you—your spouse, children, or parents—are most affected by what you say and do. Use that power wisely.

Lifters Initiate the Positive in a Negative Environment

It's one thing to be positive in a positive or neutral environment. It's another to be an instrument of change in a negative environment. Yet that's what lifters try to do. Sometimes that requires a kind word, other times it takes a servant's action, and occasionally it calls for creativity.

American revolutionary Ben Franklin told in his autobiography about asking a favor to create a positive connection in a negative environment. In 1736, Franklin was being considered for a position as clerk of the general assembly. Only one person stood in the way of his nomination—a powerful man who did not like Franklin.

Franklin wrote, "Having heard that he had in his library a certain very scarce book, I wrote a note to him, expressing my desire of perusing that book and requesting he would do me the favor of lending it to me." The man was flattered and delighted by the request. He loaned Franklin the book, and the two became lifelong friends.

How can you initiate a relationship with an unlikely friend?

_____

_____

_____

Lifters Understand Life Is Not a Dress Rehearsal

Here's a quote I've always loved: "I expect to pass through this world but once. Any good therefore that I can do, or any kindness that I can show to any fellow creature, let me do it now. Let me not defer or neglect it, for I shall not pass this way again."[5] People who lift others don't wait until tomorrow or some other "better" day to help people. They act now!

APPLYING THE ELEVATOR PRINCIPLE

1. Do people who don't intentionally work at adding value to others automatically become subtracters? Why? What is the main difference between adders and subtracters? Explain.

_____

_____

_____

2. Why do people become dividers? Is unforgiveness ever an issue? (George Herbert says, "He who cannot forgive others breaks the bridge over which he must pass himself.") Is the choice to become a divider permanent? What actions at work or home have you engaged in that could be seen as divisive? How can you be sure to avoid such behavior in the future?

_____

_____

_____

3. Do you agree that the small things a person does can easily lift or lower others? How do small things affect a child? Are parents responsible for lifting up their children or toughening them up? Explain. If you are a parent, do you find yourself more often encouraging your children or disciplining them? If change would be beneficial, what things might you do to improve?

_____

_____

_____

4. How can a person lift or lower others without saying a word? How might a person's facial expressions either encourage or discourage others? How would you describe your natural facial expression? How would others describe it? How can you make it more open and encouraging?

_____

_____

_____

5. What is the main difference between adders and multipliers? Can anyone become a multiplier? Explain. How often have you multiplied value in another person's life? What must you do to become a better multiplier?

_____

_____

_____

Summary

In relationships, receiving is easy. Giving is much more difficult. It's similar to the difference between building something and tearing it down. It takes a skilled craftsman much time and energy to build a beautiful chair. It takes no skill whatsoever to smash that chair in a matter of moments.

However, everyone is capable of becoming a person who lifts up others. You don't have to be rich. You don't have to be a genius. You don't have to have it all together. You do have to care about people and initiate lifting activities. Don't let another day go by without lifting up the people in your life. Doing that will positively change the relationships you already have and open you up to many more.

THE CONNECTION QUESTION
ARE WE WILLING
TO FOCUS ON OTHERS?

Strangers are
what friends are made of.

—CULLEN HIGHTOWER

All human beings possess a desire to connect with other people. It doesn't matter how young or old, introverted or extroverted, rich or poor, learned or uneducated they happen to be. The need for connection is sometimes motivated by the desire for love, but it can just as easily be prompted by feelings of loneliness, the need for acceptance, the quest for fulfillment, or the desire to achieve in business.

How can we fulfill our desire for relationships? What is the best way to get started? In other words, how can we connect? The answer is that we must stop thinking about ourselves and begin focusing on the people with whom we desire to build relationships. That's why the connection question asks, "Are we willing to focus on others?"

To increase your chances of connecting with another person, you need to understand and learn the following six People Principles:

The Big Picture Principle: The entire population of the world—with one minor exception—is composed of others.

The Exchange Principle: Instead of putting others in their place, we must put ourselves in their place.

The Learning Principle: Each person we meet has the potential to teach us something.

The Charisma Principle: People are interested in the person who is interested in them.

The Number 10 Principle: Believing the best in people usually brings the best out of people.

The Confrontation Principle: Caring for people should precede confronting people.

When you stop worrying so much about yourself and start looking at others and what they desire, you build a bridge to other people. And you become the kind of person others want to be around. These are the keys to connecting.

THE BIG PICTURE PRINCIPLE

THE ENTIRE POPULATION OF THE WORLD— WITH ONE MINOR EXCEPTION— IS COMPOSED OF OTHERS

A person first starts to live when he can live outside himself.

—ALBERT EINSTEIN

THE QUESTION I MUST ASK MYSELF:
DO I HAVE A HARD TIME PUTTING
OTHERS FIRST?

W hat does it take to change people's perspective and help them see the big picture for the first time in their lives? Sometimes it's getting married. Other times it's getting divorced. Or having a child. The bottom line is that people need to understand that everything is not about them.

READING BETWEEN THE LINES

I recently read an article about actress Angelina Jolie. The catalyst for her change in perspective was a script. Jolie, who won an Oscar in 1999 for her role in *Girl, Interrupted*, could have been the poster girl for a life adrift. The child of actors Jon Voight and Marcheline Bertrand, she had grown up in Hollywood and indulged in many of its excesses. She was called a "wild child." And she was well known for drug usage, outrageous behavior, and sometimes self-destructive actions. She was convinced she would die young.

"There was a time where I never had a sense of purpose, never felt useful as a person," says Jolie. "I think a lot of people have that feeling—wanting to kill yourself or take drugs or numb yourself out because you can't shut it off or you just feel bad and you don't know what it's from."[1]

Success in movies did little to help her. "I felt so off balance all the time," admits Jolie. "I remember one of the most upsetting times in my life was after I had attained success, financial stability, and I was in love, and I thought, 'I have everything that they say you should have to be happy and I'm not happy.'"[2]

But then she read the script for *Beyond Borders*, the story of a woman living a life of privilege who discovers the plight of refugees and orphans around the world. Jolie recalls, "Something in me really wanted to understand what the film was about, these people in the world, all these displaced people and war and famine and refugees."[3] For a year she traveled around the world with UN workers. "I got my greatest life education and changed drastically," she observes. She visited camps in Sierra Leone, Tanzania, Côte d'Ivoire, Cambodia, Pakistan, Namibia, and Thailand. Her entire perspective changed. She realized that the entire world was made up of other people, many of whom were in dire circumstances, many of whom she could help.

When the United Nations High Commissioner for Refugees asked her to become a goodwill ambassador in 2001, she was happy to do it. She also began donating money to help refugees and orphans, including $3 million to the UN's refugee program. (She says she makes a "stupid amount of money" to act in movies.)[4] And she adopted a Cambodian orphan, Maddox. Recently *Worth* magazine listed her as one of the twenty-five most influential philanthropists in the world. She estimates that she gives almost a third of her income to charity.[5]

Jolie puts it all into perspective: "You could die tomorrow and you've done a few movies, won some awards—that doesn't mean anything. But if you've built schools or raised a child or done something to make things better for other people, then it just feels better. Life is better."[6] Why does she feel that way? Because she finally gets the big picture. She stopped focusing on herself and began putting other people ahead of herself.

What experiences in your life have given you a big-picture perspective?

_____

_____

_____

From Here Everything Looks Different

When it comes to winning with people, everything begins with the ability to think about people other than ourselves. That is the most basic principle in building relationships. I know that may sound like common sense, yet not everyone gets the big picture or practices unselfishness. Instead, too many people act more like toddlers, whose perspective is something like this:

> If I like it, it's mine.
> If I can take it away from you, it's mine.
> If I had it a while ago, it's mine.
> If I say it is mine, it's mine.
> If it looks like mine, it's mine.
> If I saw it first, it's mine.
> If you're having fun with it, it's definitely mine.
> If you lay it down, it's mine.
> If it is broken, it's yours.[7]

People who remain self-centered and self-serving will always have a hard time getting along with others. To help them break that pattern of living, they need the big picture, which requires three things:

1. Perspective

People who lack perspective are like Lucy in the *Peanuts* comic strip by Charles Schulz. In one strip while Lucy swings on the playground, Charlie Brown reads to her, "It says here that the world revolves around the sun once a year."

Lucy stops abruptly and responds, "The world revolves around the sun? Are you sure? I thought it revolved around me."

Of course, lack of perspective is usually much more subtle than that. I know it was for me. Early in my career as a pastor, as I led others, the question I continually asked myself was, *How can these people help* me? I wanted to use people to help me accomplish my goals. It took me a couple of years to realize that I had everything backward and should have been asking, *How can I help these people?* When I did, not only was I able to help others, but I was also helped. I learned what William B. Given Jr. meant when he observed, "Whenever you are too selfishly looking out for your own interest, you have only one person working for you—yourself. When you help a dozen other people with their problems, you have a dozen people working with you."

Who are you currently helping? What are your motives for helping them?

_____

_____

_____

Most of the time, what we worry about is small in the big scheme of things. Many years ago John McKay, former head football coach of USC, wanted to help his team recover after being humiliated 51–0 by Notre Dame. McKay went into the locker room and saw a group of beaten, worn-out, and thoroughly depressed young football players who were not accustomed to losing. He stood up on a bench and said, "Men, let's keep this in perspective. There are 800 million Chinese people who don't even know this game was played."

The entire world—with one minor exception—is composed of others. And most of the people in the world don't know you and never will. Most of the ones you do know probably have greater needs and problems than you do. You can choose to ignore them and focus on yourself, or you can get over yourself and learn to put other people first.

2. Maturity

My granddaughters, Hannah and Maddie, are three years old as I write this. I just spent a wonderful Thanksgiving with them. It was a joy watching them play and doing things for them. But I have to say one thing about them. In all the time we were together, they never once asked, "What can I do for you, Papa?" That's okay for a three-year-old. It's not okay at age thirty!

We often expect maturity to come with age, but the truth is, sometimes age comes alone. An attitude that says, "Save time—see it my way," can be lifelong unless a person chooses to fight against it.

How would you define maturity?

_____

_____

_____

Several years ago, author and consultant Bob Buford wrote an excellent book titled *Halftime*. Its thesis is that as they approach middle age, many people reach a time of uneasiness that comes from wanting greater meaning in their lives. He defines that as *halftime*. He says that most people try to do in the second half of their lives what they did in the first half—only more so. Instead, the key to a successful halftime is to take stock, focus on your area of strength, and make giving to others your goal.

Why would the second half of your life be the ideal time to focus on using your strengths and giving to others?

_____

_____

_____

Here is how Bob describes the difference in attitude between people before and after halftime:

While the first-half self is small, the second-half self is large. The first-half self winds inward, wrapping tighter and tighter around itself. The second-half winds outward, unraveling itself from the paralysis of a tightly-wound spring.

The small self contains only you. It is basically alienated, alone, and pathologically individualistic. The larger self is whole because it is bonded with something transcendent. Self-transcendence has legs; it goes the distance and completes the race.

Bob is describing real maturity. It is knowing that the world does not revolve around you. It is the ability to see the big picture.

3. Responsibility

You may have observed that marriage has a way of magnifying an irresponsible person's lack of responsibility. Anyone who goes into marriage expecting to maintain the same level of freedom he had when he was single is going to put his marriage at risk. To make a marriage work, both partners must be responsible. Marriage relationships mature when each partner stops asking, *What can my spouse do for me?* and starts taking the responsibility to ask, *What can I do for my spouse?*

Leadership puts similar demands on people. Accepting leadership responsibilities for the first time exposes an individual's level of maturity and sense of responsibility. Irresponsible leaders have a "me first" attitude and use their position for personal benefit. Responsible leaders have an "others first" attitude and use their position for serving people, taking responsibility, being an example, giving others credit, and mending relationships. Good leaders understand that for the team to succeed, they must put others first.

In your experience, do most leaders put others first? How does their "me first" or "others first" attitude affect the group?

_____

_____

_____

OPENING YOUR EYES TO THE BIG PICTURE

If you would like to improve your ability to see the big picture and put others first, then do the following:

Get Out of Your "Own Little World"

To change focus, people need to get out of their own little world. If you have a narrow view of people, go places you have never gone, meet the kind of people you do not know, and do things you have not done before. It will change your perspective, as it has done mine.

Check Your Ego at the Door

Have you ever spent much time talking to someone with a big ego? The good news is that such people never talk much about others. (Maybe that is because they're always "me-deep" in conversation!) The bad news is that if you don't want to hear about them, you're going to be bored very quickly.

An egotist can be described *not* as a person who thinks too much of himself, but as someone who thinks too little of other people. We often mistakenly believe that the opposite of love is hate. But I believe that's incorrect. The opposite of loving others is being self-centered. If your focus is always on yourself, you'll never be able to build positive relationships.

Do you agree that the opposite of loving others is being self-centered? Explain.

_____

_____

_____

Applying the Big Picture Principle

1. At what phase of life do many people begin learning to think about others? What events often prompt people to start putting others first? What happens when a person tries to skip the life lessons that inspire other-mindedness? What happens to people whose focus, time, and energy are spent entirely on themselves, even in their later years?

_____

_____

_____

2. What is the main difference between people with big egos and those with great confidence? Why is a big ego undesirable? Why is confidence desirable? Do you think ego and lack of confidence are related? Explain.

_____

_____

_____

3. Describe your experiences with traveling. Which destinations have been similar to your own environment? Have you traveled to places with cultures very different from your own? Which specific destinations made you most uncomfortable? Why? Did you learn anything from traveling there? Where would you like to travel in the future? Why?

_____

_____

_____

4. How would you define *fulfillment*? Can a person with no meaningful relationships be fulfilled? Explain your opinion. How does your opinion affect the effort you put into relationship building?

_____

_____

_____

5. Think about the most important relationships in your life. Have you always displayed appropriate maturity and responsibility in them? If not, how can you work to make things right? What should you change about yourself so that your behavior is appropriate in the future?

_____

_____

_____

Summary

Antislavery reformer Henry Ward Beecher said, "No man is more cheated than the selfish man." That is true because he separates himself from what's most important in life: people. If you want to live a fulfilling life, you need healthy relationships. And to build those kinds of relationships, you need to get over yourself. Embrace the Big Picture Principle and remind yourself that the entire population of the world—with one minor exception—is composed of others.

THE EXCHANGE PRINCIPLE

INSTEAD OF PUTTING OTHERS IN THEIR PLACE, WE MUST PUT OURSELVES IN THEIR PLACE

Sometimes when you give someone a piece of your mind,
you lose your own peace of mind.

> THE QUESTION I MUST ASK MYSELF:
> DO I TRY TO SEE THINGS
> FROM OTHERS' POINT OF VIEW?

Since 1996 I have been teaching leadership internationally to Christian leaders through a nonprofit organization I founded called EQUIP. It is one of my greatest joys, and I believe that its accomplishments will be a major part of my legacy. Everyone on the EQUIP team is working hard to achieve the goal of raising up and equipping one million leaders by 2008.

One place where my messages have been received well is the Philippines. When I first began teaching there, I was teaching leadership almost exclusively to Filipino pastors and other Christian leaders. However, my books and other materials started to spread beyond the Christian community into the business world. That didn't come as a big surprise because a similar thing had already happened in the United States and in several African countries. What surprised me was that the Philippine government became interested in my leadership teachings.

The country's secretary of the interior contacted me to say that the government wanted to send a copy of *The 21 Irrefutable Laws of Leadership* to every mayor in the Philippines. Then later he let me know that they also wanted to send a copy to every town council member in the country. It was very humbling to think that ideas I had put into writing might be shared with so many people of influence. I was glad to give my permission.

A VISIT WITH THE PRESIDENT

In January 2003, I was invited to meet with the president of the Philippines, Gloria Macapagal-Arroyo. It was a great honor. I found the president to be very sharp, very warm, and very intelligent. (She has a Ph.D. in economics.) We talked about leadership, and to my surprise and delight, she pulled out a well-worn copy of *The 21 Irrefutable Laws of Leadership*. She told me she was using it to mentor her cabinet. For a while she asked me questions about leadership, and we discussed various points from the book. It was a totally enjoyable experience.

As our time came to a close, I decided to talk to her about something that had made an impression on me. In my travels around the world, I had observed that in developing countries, many leaders take advantage of their people. Those with power take advantage of the powerless. That trend is at its worst in countries with dictators, but it seems to happen everywhere at every level of leadership: the poorer the country, the greater the abuse.

I shared my observation with the president and said that I saw many leaders using their positions to add value to themselves instead of adding value to others. And I added, "You seem to be a leader who really wants to add value to others."

"Oh, yes," she answered, "my only agenda is to help the people of my country. I am considering serving only one term in office so that I can focus on service instead of politics." From what I have seen and read, she is adding value and serving well.

THE POWER OF PERSPECTIVE

Success can bring many things: power, privilege, fame, and wealth. But no matter what else it brings, with success come options. How we use those options reveals our character. Wealthy people can use their resources to benefit others or only themselves. Famous people can use their notoriety to model good character or to selfishly serve themselves. Leaders can make decisions that affect others positively or negatively. It's up to them.

What types of options come with success? What are some wise and unwise choices you've seen leaders make?

_____

_____

_____

At the heart of the matter is whether people desire to use their power to put others in their place or to put themselves in others' place. I believe that President Macapagal-Arroyo tries to see things from the perspective of her people and acts accordingly.

Seeing things from another person's point of view doesn't come naturally to everyone. Here's what I have discovered about the Exchange Principle:

We Naturally Do Not See Ourselves and Others from the Same Perspective

We do not look at ourselves and others in the same way. People naturally see themselves in the light of their intentions, but they measure others according to their actions. Or to put it the way poet Henry Wadsworth Longfellow did: "We judge ourselves by what we feel capable of doing, while others judge us by what we have already done."

We naturally try to see ourselves in the most positive light. And that's okay as long as we're being honest with ourselves. But we really ought to give others the same benefit of the doubt that we give ourselves.

When We Fail to See Things from the Perspective of Others, We Fail in Our Relationships

Much of the conflict we experience in relationships comes from our failure to see things from the other person's perspective, as the following joke illustrates:

A man in a hot air balloon realized he was lost. He reduced altitude and spotted a woman below. He descended a bit more and shouted, "Excuse me, can you help me? I promised a friend I would meet him an hour ago, but I don't know where I am." The woman below replied, "You're in a hot air balloon hovering approximately 30 feet above the ground. You're between 40 and 41 degrees north altitude and between 59 and 60 degrees west longitude."

"You must be an engineer," said the balloonist.

"I am," replied the woman, "How did you know?"

"Well," answered the balloonist, "everything you told me is technically correct, but I've no idea what to make of your information, and the fact is, I'm still lost. Frankly you've not been much help at all. If anything, you've delayed my trip."

The woman below responded, "You must be in management."

"I am," replied the balloonist, "but how did you know?"

"Well," said the woman, "you don't know where you are or where you're going. You have risen to where you are due to a large quantity of hot air. You made a promise, which you've no idea how to keep, and you expect people beneath you to solve your problems. The fact is, you are in exactly the same position you were in before we met, but now, somehow, you've managed to make it my fault."

How often have you found yourself in conflict with another person because you see things one way and he sees them another? Think about it. If you're married, don't you continually face potential conflict because of the way men and women naturally see things differently? If you have children, doesn't a lot of the friction occur because they don't see things the way you do? Even in a really positive working environment, people don't see everything eye to eye. (Just remember this: before you have an argument with your boss, take a good look at both sides—his side and the outside.) Seriously, though, I believe that if people made the effort to see things from others' point of view, 80 percent of our relational conflict would disappear.

What questions can you ask to gain a better understanding of someone else's point of view?

_____

_____

_____

Learning to See Things from Others' Perspective Helps Us Succeed in Our Relationships

I read this saying in a sales journal: "If you would sell John Smith what John Smith buys, then you must see John Smith through John Smith's eyes." The concept is so simple that we think it's too obvious. Yet many people don't practice it. They're so busy putting others in their place that they don't make the effort to put themselves in someone else's place.

HOW TO MAKE THE EXCHANGE

How do you become better at making the exchange, at seeing things from another person's perspective? Start by doing these four things:

1. Leave "Your Place" and Visit "Their Place"

The best way to keep from stepping on other people's toes is to put yourself in their shoes. In the 1930s, American Airways, which later became American Airlines, had a tremendous problem with complaints from passengers about lost luggage. LaMotte Cohn, general manager of the airline at that time, tried to get his station managers to overcome this issue, but he saw little progress. Finally he came upon an idea to help the airline's personnel to see things from their customers' point of view. Cohn asked all of the station managers from across the country to fly to company headquarters for a meeting. Then he made sure that every manager's luggage was lost in transit. Afterward, the airline suddenly made a huge leap of efficiency in that area.

Do whatever you can to change your perspective. Listen to people's concerns. Study their culture or profession. Read in their areas of interest. Or literally visit their place—their home, office, neighborhood, or region. You may be surprised by how it alters your thinking. You may find out, as President Harry Truman did, that "when we understand the other fellow's viewpoint . . . understand what he is trying to do . . . nine times out of ten he is trying to do right."

What is the most common complaint your team receives? How are you trying to improve your service or job skills? How will you know when the situation has improved?

_____

_____

_____

2. Acknowledge that the Other Person Has a Valid Viewpoint

People's belief systems and personal experiences are diverse and complex. And even if you do work to see things from another person's point of view, there will still be differences of opinion. That's all right. My viewpoint isn't right just because it's mine. If I work to find the legitimacy of another person's point of view, it will stretch my thinking. And as jurist Oliver Wendell Holmes said, "Once a mind has been stretched by a new idea, it never returns to its original shape."

Who and what views have stretched your mind?

_____

_____

_____

3. Check Your Attitude

When it comes to seeing things from another person's point of view, attitude is huge. It is always easy to see both sides of an issue that you are not particularly concerned about. It becomes much harder when you have a vested interest in it. When that's the case, you are often more concerned with getting your way than making a way to connect with others. At the core of that is whether you are willing to change. When you don't want to change, you look for differences in others. When you are willing to change, you look for similarities.

Are you willing to adjust to others or do you expect them to adjust to you? Explain.

_____

_____

_____

4. Ask Others What They Would Do in Your Situation

The key to the Exchange Principle is empathy. And when you have empathy with others' point of view, it becomes much easier to connect with them. Why? Because they know that you care. Sometimes the easiest way to do that is to simply ask.

If you put yourself in the place of others instead of putting others in their place, it changes the way you see life, and it changes the way you live it. Dan Clark recalls that when he was a teenager, he and his father once stood in line to buy tickets for the circus. As they waited, they noticed the family immediately in front of them. The parents were holding hands, and they had eight children in tow, all well behaved and all probably under the age of twelve. Based on their clean but simple clothing, he suspected that they didn't have a lot of money. The kids jabbered about the exciting things they expected to see, and he could tell that the circus was going to be a new adventure for them.

As the couple approached the counter, the attendant asked how many tickets they wanted. The man proudly responded, "Please let me buy eight children's tickets and two adult tickets so I can take my family to the circus."

When the attendant quoted the price, the man's wife let go of his hand, and her head drooped. The man leaned a little closer and asked, "How much did you say?" The attendant again quoted the price. The man obviously didn't have enough money. He looked crushed.

Clark says that his father watched all of this, put his hand in his pocket, pulled out a twenty-dollar bill, and dropped it on the ground. His father then reached down, picked up the bill, tapped the man on the shoulder, and said, "Excuse me, sir, this fell out of your pocket."

The man knew exactly what was going on. He looked straight into Clark's father's eyes, took his hand, shook it, and with a tear streaming down his cheek, replied, "Thank you, thank you, sir. This really means a lot to me and my family."

Clark and his father went back to their car and drove home. They didn't have enough money to go to the circus that night, but it didn't matter. Because they had put themselves into the place of others, they had done something more important.

APPLYING THE EXCHANGE PRINCIPLE

1. What kinds of positive things can happen to people's perspective of others when they travel to foreign places and become exposed to other cultures? What kinds of changes might occur? How can preconceptions work against those positive changes?

_____

_____

_____

2. What issues prevent people from wanting to "get outside themselves" and see things from another person's point of view? What obstacles do you face? What have you done in the past to overcome them? What might you do in the future to increase your ability to see things from others' point of view?

_____

_____

_____

3. How would you describe your general attitude toward people? Do you automatically assume that others have a valid point of view, or do you always believe you are right? Explain. If you need to do better about giving people the benefit of the doubt, how will you work to improve?

_____

_____

_____

4. What happens in relationships when someone puts others "in their place"? How can someone repair a relationship that has experienced that dynamic?

_____

_____

_____

5. How good are you at focusing on others? How often do you ask people to share their perspective on an issue? How frequently do you ask others what they desire? Are you generally focused on your agenda, or is seeing things from others' perspective a high priority in your life? Would those closest to you agree with your assessment?

_____

_____

_____

Summary

Educator and agricultural chemist George Washington Carver made an incredible observation: "How far you go in life depends on your being tender with the young, compassionate with the aged, sympathetic with the striving, and tolerant of the weak and strong. Because someday in life you will have been all of these." Our treatment of others always results from our perspective of them. If you take time to get to know the people around you, I can almost guarantee that your environment will become even more pleasant.

THE LEARNING PRINCIPLE

EACH PERSON WE MEET
HAS THE POTENTIAL
TO TEACH US SOMETHING

*There are some people
that if they don't know, you can't tell them.*

—LOUIS ARMSTRONG

THE QUESTION I MUST ASK MYSELF:
DO I APPROACH PEOPLE
WITH A DESIRE TO LEARN FROM THEM?

61

You would recognize him if you saw him. A well-known character actor, he has appeared in dozens of movies and on numerous television shows. He appeared as Guido the pimp in *Risky Business*. He was Tommy Lee Jones's sidekick in *The Fugitive*. He portrayed the traitor Cypher in *The Matrix*. And he played Ralphie on *The Sopranos*. To his friends, he's known as Joey Pants. His real name is Joe Pantoliano.

Joe was born and grew up in Hoboken, New Jersey. It was a tough area. He says his role models were the local wiseguys—the gangsters who worked with the Mafia. His parents moved a lot; both were gamblers and, as a result, not very good at paying their bills. When Joe was nine or ten, his mother was working as a bookie to earn money, and she used Joe as her runner. Joey Pants seemed to be destined for a life of crime.

WISEGUY AT HOME

That fate was seemingly sealed when a distant cousin, Florio Isabella, got out of prison and moved into the Pantoliano household when Joe was thirteen. Florie, as he was called, was a career criminal. As a boy growing up in Little Italy in New York City, Florie delivered the heroin that his parents prepared in their one-room apartment. By age twelve, he was selling the narcotic. He had spent twenty-one years of his life in prison. Besides drug trafficking, he had committed armed robbery and other serious crimes, including hijacking the Hoboken Ferry.

Joe recalls, "He immediately violated his parole by getting back into the life [of crime] with some gangsters called the Paradise Brothers. I remember he made $50,000 in cash."[1] But after one of the Paradise brothers was killed gangland style, Florie got to thinking. The fork in the road for Florie became a fork in the road for Joe, though he didn't recognize it at the time. Florie could have taken on Joe as his criminal protégé. That's the way many criminals get started. But the old gangster did something different. Joe remembers, "He always said, 'Every move I made was always the wrong one. And that ain't going to be you.' He was the only one who had faith in me and encouraged me to follow my heart."[2]

Joe's heart was set on acting. But when he summoned the courage to tell people about it, friends and family alike ridiculed him. "Who do you think you are," his mother told him, "you wanna be an actor? People like us don't become actors. People like us don't go to college. People like us don't get ahead. Don't shake the boat, Joey."[3]

But Florie—the most unlikely person in his life—taught him to be different from the rest of his family and the friends he grew up with. Florie got him connected to his first acting teacher. When Joe was ready to leave home and move to New York City, Florie not only encouraged him but also gave him money. He drove Joe to work the day he played in his first movie—as an extra in *The Valachi Papers*. Most important, Florie kept him away from the life of crime that could have brought Joe easy money the first seven years he struggled as an actor. "Had not Florio Isabella, my other father, my honorary stepfather and third cousin to my mother, stepped on to the scene in time," says Joe, "[my] return address would be Attica, New York," meaning the prison.[4]

"In the end," observes Joe, "I am left with the tragic fact that the one person in my life who made me feel I could be something did some very terrible things. Florie would, by some standards, be considered a horrible person, who may have tried to rectify his deeds through helping encourage my confidence and success with his unconditional love. He was the sweetest wiseguy I ever knew."[5]

Describe your most unique or unlikely friend. What have you learned from him or her?

_____

_____

_____

WHAT'S YOUR ATTITUDE?

The truth is that all of us, like Joe Pantoliano, can learn things in unlikely places—and from unlikely people. Everybody has something to share, something to teach us. But that's true only if we have the right attitude.

What kind of attitude do you have when it comes to learning from others? All people fall into one of the categories described by the following statements:

No One Can Teach Me Anything—Arrogant Attitude

I think we sometimes assume that ignorance is the greatest enemy of teachability. However, that really has little to do with teachability. Haven't you known some highly educated and highly successful people who do not want to hear the suggestions or opinions of anyone else? Some people think they know it all! A person who creates a large, successful organization may think he can't learn from people who run a smaller one. A person who receives a doctorate can become unreceptive to instruction from anyone else because she is now considered an expert. Another person who is the most experienced in a company or department may not listen to the ideas of someone younger.

Such people don't realize how much they are hurting themselves. The reality is that no one is too old, too smart, or too successful to learn something new. The only thing that can come between a person and the ability to learn and improve is a bad attitude.

Someone Can Teach Me Everything—Naive Attitude

People who realize that they have room to grow often seek a mentor. That's usually a good thing. However, it's naive for individuals to think they can learn everything they need to know from just one person. People don't need *a* mentor—they need *many* mentors. I've learned so much from so many people. Les Stobbe taught me how to write. My brother Larry is my business mentor. I've learned a lot about communication from Andy Stanley. Tom Mullins models relationships for me. If I tried to include all the people who have taught me over the years, I'd fill page after page with names.

Everyone Can Teach Me Something—Teachable Attitude

The people who learn the most aren't necessarily the ones who spend time with the smartest people. They are the ones with a teachable attitude. Every person has something to share—a lesson learned, an observation, a life experience. We just need to be willing to listen. In fact, people often teach us things when they don't intend to do so. Ask any parents and you will find out that they learned things from their children— even when their kids were infants incapable of communicating a single word. The only time people can't teach us things is when we are unwilling to learn.

I'm not saying that every person you meet *will* teach you something. All I'm saying is that people have the potential to do so—if you'll let them.

HOW TO LEARN FROM OTHERS

If you have a teachable attitude—or you are willing to adopt one—you will be positioned well to learn from others. Then all you will need to do is to take the following five steps:

1. Make Learning Your Passion

If you desire to keep growing, you cannot sit back in a comfort zone. You need to make learning your goal. Do that and you will never run out of gas mentally, and your motivation will be strong. Don't worry about having people to teach you. Greek philosopher Plato said, "When the pupil is ready, the teacher will appear."

What is your attitude toward learning? Has your past experience with school colored it?

_____

_____

_____

2. Value People

In 1976, I had been in my career for seven years, and I felt successful. In those days, churches were often judged by the success of their Sunday school programs, and the church I led had the fastest-growing program in the state of Ohio. And by then my church had grown to be the largest in my denomination. But I still wanted to learn. That year I signed up to attend a conference. There were three speakers that I wanted to hear. They were older, more successful, and more experienced than I.

During the conference, one of the sessions was an idea exchange where anybody could talk. I figured it would be a waste of time, and I was going to skip it, but my curiosity got the best of me. It turned out to be a real eye-opener. Person after person shared what was working in his organization, and I sat there scribbling notes and jotting down ideas. It turned out that I learned more during that session than in all the others combined.

That surprised me, and later I realized why. Before that conference, I thought only older, more successful people could teach me anything. I had walked into that room placing very little value on the other people there. And that was a wrong attitude. People don't learn from people they don't value. I determined to change my thinking from that day forward.

Have you ever been surprised to learn from someone? Explain.

_____

_____

_____

3. Develop Relationships with Growth Potential

It's true that everyone has *something* to teach us, but that doesn't mean anyone can teach us *everything* we want to learn. We need to find people who are especially likely to help us grow—experts in our field, creative thinkers who will stretch us mentally, achievers who will inspire us to go to the next level. Learning is often the reward for spending time with remarkable people. Who they are and what they know rub off. As Donald Clifton and Paula Nelson, authors of *Soar with Your Strengths*, observe, "Relationships help us define who we are and what we become."

List your mentors (or potential mentors). Why have you chosen each person to learn from?

_____

_____

_____

4. Identify People's Uniqueness and Strengths

Philosopher-poet Ralph Waldo Emerson remarked, "I have never met a man who was not my superior in some particular." People grow best in their areas of strength—and can learn the most from another person's area of strength. For that reason, you can't be indiscriminate in choosing the people you seek out to teach you.

In the mid-1970s, I identified the top ten church leaders in the nation, and I tried to get an appointment for lunch with each of them. I even offered them one hundred dollars for an hour of their time—that was a half week's pay back then. Some were willing to meet me. Others weren't. I was extremely grateful to the ones who did.

My wife and I didn't have much money then, and these leaders lived all over the country, so we planned our vacations for several years around these visits. Why would I go to such lengths to meet these people? Because I was dying to learn the unique skills and strengths they possessed. The meetings made a huge difference in my life. And do you know what? Connection with great men and women continues to affect my life. Every month I try to meet with someone I admire and from whom I want to learn.

Is there someone you would love to meet and learn from? What steps can you take to learn from that person?

_____

_____

_____

5. Ask Questions

The first year I was in college, I took a part-time job at a locker plant in Circleville, Ohio. It was a place where cows were slaughtered and the meat was stored in giant refrigerated lockers. My job was to haul freshly processed meat to the refrigeration areas and to retrieve orders of meat for customers.

Anytime I'm exposed to something new—and this was a new area for me—I try to learn about it. And the best way to learn is to watch and ask questions. I had been working for about two weeks when Pense, an old guy who had worked there for years, pulled me aside and said, "Son, let me tell you something. You ask too many questions. I've been working here for a long time. I kill cows. That's all I do—and that's all I'm gonna do. The more you know, the more they expect you to do." I had a hard time understanding why anybody *wouldn't* want to learn and grow. But obviously he was committed not to change.

The person who asks the right questions learns the most, and learning begins with listening. But it doesn't end there. Theology professor Hans Küng asserted, "Understanding someone properly involves learning from him, and learning from someone properly involves changing oneself." Change is always the goal of learning. You cannot have growth without change.

APPLYING THE LEARNING PRINCIPLE

1. How open are most people to learning from others? What kind of attitude do most people possess? Do you think most people quickly prejudge whether they can learn something from another individual? If so, do you think it's done intentionally or unintentionally? Explain. What factors come into play (such as appearance, position, income, race, age, etc.) concerning whether a person has something to offer? What prejudices do you think *you* might possess? How can you change them?

_____

_____

_____

2. Two kinds of learning are mentioned in the chapter: one has to do with being _open_ to learning from anyone at any time; the other has to do with being _strategic_ about how we learn and from whom. What kinds of benefits are you likely to receive from each? What are the greatest challenges you may face for each? Which one is more appealing to you personally?

_____

_____

_____

3. What is your philosophy concerning learning and personal growth? Had you previously given it much thought? How would you say it differs from the ideas stated in the chapter? What new ideas can you easily adopt and make your own?

_____

_____

_____

4. What kind of roles have mentors played in your personal growth so far in your life? Describe a key person from your past who taught you something significant. Who currently helps you to grow? Have you sought out a single mentor to guide you, or do you try to connect with several people? Who in your current circle of acquaintances has expertise in an area that can help you? What can you do to enlist that help?

_____

_____

_____

5. How are you when it comes to asking questions? When you meet people for the first time, do you ask questions to get to know them better? Do some of your questions prompt conversation that will teach you something? How about when you get ready to meet with a mentor or teacher: Do you prepare questions in advance to make the best use of the time?

_____

_____

_____

Summary

This chapter has focused primarily on the importance of learning from others. But you never know who might be listening and learning from you. Every day we have an opportunity to invest in others. Be open to helping those around you while continually maintaining a teachable attitude. A life of continual growth never gets old.

THE CHARISMA PRINCIPLE

PEOPLE ARE INTERESTED IN THE PERSON WHO IS INTERESTED IN THEM

You can make more friends in two months by becoming interested in other people than you can in two years by trying to get other people interested in you.

—DALE CARNEGIE

THE QUESTION I MUST ASK MYSELF:
DO I USUALLY FOCUS ON OTHERS
AND THEIR INTERESTS OR ON MY OWN?

I n August 2003, Margaret and I were booked to go on a Seabourn cruise in the Mediterranean. When we arrived at the check-in area and were waiting to be helped, a woman who was just a little bit older than we were came up and introduced herself.

"Hi, I'm Phyllis," she said with a brilliant smile. "What are your names?" We introduced ourselves. "It's so nice to meet you," she said. "I'm looking forward to getting to know you better. I'll let you check in. See you tonight at dinner."

"What an engaging person," Margaret said as we checked in and found out where our stateroom was.

By the time we'd unpacked later that afternoon, I'd forgotten about Phyllis. But when we went down to dinner, there she was talking to people. When she saw us, she smiled and came over to say hello.

"John and Margaret," she said, "this is my husband, Stanley," and immediately she began to engage us in conversation. We ended up eating dinner together.

"What do you do?" she asked.

"I'm an author and conference speaker," I answered.

"That sounds so interesting. Tell me about it."

I told her about my background and some of my experiences as she asked questions. Then she engaged Margaret in conversation, and soon they were talking about art and antiques.

Over the next couple of days, I watched as Phyllis and Stanley introduced themselves to the 120 passengers on the ship and connected with them. I noticed the effort Phyllis put into making people feel good about themselves. She initiated conversation, and when someone wanted to talk about her, she quickly turned the conversation back to him/her.

Phyllis knew everybody's name and had something nice to say about each person. After a couple of days, people walked around the ship looking for her. She was the Pied Piper. Everybody fell in love with her. In one of our conversations, I found out from her that she and Stanley were retired, and they were spending their retirement time taking cruises and meeting people. They seemed to be having a wonderful time.

As the cruise wound down, I told Phyllis how much Margaret and I appreciated her, and let her know we'd love to stay in touch with her. She reached into a pocket and pulled out a business card that read,

Phyllis and Stanley Hughes
Your Cruisin' Friends

and beneath it was the ship's logo along with the couple's home address and phone number. Since that cruise, Phyllis has written us and extended an invitation to visit her and Stanley in Florida.

Phyllis Hughes was as charismatic a person as I've ever met. She was a master at connecting with people. What was her secret? It's the same thing I was taught in 1963 when my father sent me to my first Dale Carnegie class: If you want to connect with others, focus on them, not on yourself.

Do you know a "Phyllis"? How do you feel when you are around this person?

_____

_____

_____

Six Ways to Make People Like You
(with Thanks to Dale Carnegie)

Carnegie's teachings in the class and in *How to Win Friends and Influence People* made a profound impression on me as a teenager. They had such an impact that I've worked to pattern my people skills on much of what he taught. Here are the six things Carnegie suggested, along with my explanations:

1. Become Genuinely Interested in Other People

Someone once asked Perle Mesta, the greatest Washington hostess since Dolley Madison, the secret of her success in getting so many rich and famous people to attend her parties. "It's all in the greetings and good-byes," she claimed. As her guests arrived, she met them with, "At last you're here!" As each one departed, she expressed her regrets by saying, "I'm sorry you have to leave so soon!"

For nearly twenty years, I've used the following statement as a guideline and reminder for interacting with others: people don't care how much you know until they know how much you care. It doesn't matter how much power, education, or expertise you possess; people will respond to you more favorably if you first let them know that they matter to you as individuals.

How can you show your genuine interest in others?

_____

_____

_____

2. Smile

Have you ever experienced one of those look-in-the-mirror realizations about yourself that changed the way you lived? I had one when I was in third grade. It came when I was literally standing in front of the mirror one morning. I looked at my face, and for the first time I saw it as someone else might, and I thought, *John, you are not a handsome dude.* I wondered, *What can I do to change that?* Then I smiled. And I thought, *That helps!* I've been smiling ever since.

A smile is inviting. Charlie Wetzel, my writer, once worked educational trade shows where he sold classroom supplies to teachers. When he worked in the booth, he always made it a point to smile at everyone. Most of the people walked down the aisles with their eyes focused on the various products each vendor had to offer. But Charlie says an interesting thing often happened. Many people walked down the aisle, but at the last second when they were almost past the booth, they would look up at him for a moment. More than half of those people saw his smile, made a sudden U-turn, and came back to look at his products in the booth. It was almost as though a string was attached to them and drew them back.

Charlie is not unusually handsome, so looks weren't the reason for the sudden change. Nor were his products especially flashy or colorful. It was the smile. (He even experimented to verify this. When he made eye contact without smiling, people just kept walking.) If you want to draw others to you, light up your face with a smile.

Just for today, try to smile at each person you encounter. Then record how people reacted to your smile.

_____

_____

_____

3. Remember that a Person's Name Is to Him or Her the Sweetest and Most Important Sound

When I took that first Dale Carnegie course, the instructor's emphasis on learning names really made an impression on me. And from that day forward, it became a priority for me. Over the years, I've used all kinds of tricks to remember people's names. I'll find a distinguishing characteristic on a person's face and associate that with the name. I'll do a little trick with words to remind me of a name.

When I was the pastor of a large church, I even offered to memorize the names of people willing to have a Polaroid picture taken of themselves. At one point I had about five hundred photos to memorize. I used to punch a hole in the corner of them and keep them on big rings. I remember once on a plane I had pulled a couple of the rings out of my briefcase so that I could review them and work on the names.

A fellow sitting beside me asked, "What are you doing?"

"Looking at pictures of my family," I responded without missing a beat.

"That's a *big* family," he answered.

I kept flipping through the pictures and said, "Yeah, but just wait until we have grand-children."

Are you good with names? How do you remember people's names? If you are not good at it, how will you improve?

_____

_____

_____

4. Be a Good Listener—Encourage Others to Talk about Themselves

Novelist George Eliot advised, "Try to care about something in this vast world besides the gratification of small selfish desires. Try to care for what is best in thought and action—something that is good apart from the accidents of your own lot. Look on other lives besides your own. See what their troubles are, and how they are borne."

How does one take that advice to heart? By listening! That was Phyllis Hughes's gift. She was one of the best listeners I've ever known. She reminded me a lot of my mother, Laura Maxwell. She is the best listener I've ever known. Not only has she always been there for me, but she's been a good listener for many people. Years ago when she was the librarian at Circleville Bible College, dozens of girls used to seek her out and confide in her because she cared about them and they knew she would always listen. Margaret says that ability made her a great mother-in-law.

5. Talk in Terms of the Other Person's Interests

To win in relationships, a person needs to learn to talk in terms of the other person's interests. That's true when meeting somebody for the first time, and it's true when you're building a marriage. One of the keys is what author Tony Allesandra calls the Platinum Rule. You probably know the Golden Rule: do unto others as you would have them do unto you. The Platinum Rule says, "Treat others the way *they* want to be treated." Do that, and you almost can't go wrong.

6. Make the Other Person Feel Important, and Do It Sincerely

The bottom line is that you need to make others feel important. Phyllis's charm wasn't a put-on. You could tell that she genuinely loved people. To her, everyone was important. And anyone can learn to value people, make them feel important, and display charisma. It all boils down to this: the person *without* charisma walks into a group and says, "Here I am." The person *with* charisma walks into a group and says, "There you are." Just about anybody can learn to do that.

APPLYING THE CHARISMA PRINCIPLE

1. Why do people find it so difficult to become genuinely interested in others? Has that been a problem for you? Explain.

_____

_____

_____

2. Can you think of someone you know personally who is charismatic and gifted at connecting with others? How much of that person's charm comes from natural talent and how much from learnable actions? What can you do to be more like that charismatic person?

_____

_____

_____

3. Have you ever done "homework" to find out more about someone else's interests so that you could better connect with that person? Did you find the experience pleasurable or a chore? How did it ultimately affect the relationship? How can you quickly find out about another person's interests "on the fly" when it's impossible or inappropriate to do research? What kinds of questions should you ask? How can you use observation?

_____

_____

_____

4. What can happen when one uses insincere flattery with another person to make him/her feel important? Do you find it difficult to make people feel important when you don't especially admire them? Explain. How can you find genuine ways to express appreciation in such situations? How can you work to change your attitude toward people you don't like?

_____

_____

_____

SUMMARY

Two great prime ministers in Great Britain's history are William Gladstone and Benjamin Disraeli. It's said that a young lady went to dinner with them on successive nights. When asked for her impressions of the two men, she said, "When I left the dining room after sitting next to Mr. Gladstone, I thought he was the cleverest man in England. But after sitting next to Mr. Disraeli, I thought I was the cleverest woman in England!"

Help to make others feel clever or important. Offer a sincere compliment, smile as they walk by, or just acknowledge their ideas or efforts. You impact those around you, for better or worse.

THE NUMBER 10 PRINCIPLE

Believing the Best
in People Usually Brings
the Best Out of People

Keep away from people who try to belittle your ambitions.
Small people always do that, but the really great make you feel
that you, too, can become great.

—Mark Twain

THE QUESTION I MUST ASK MYSELF:
DO I BELIEVE THE BEST OF OTHERS?

I n 1995, I saw the movie *Dangerous Minds,* an inspiring tale of a teacher who wanted
to make a difference in the lives of her teenage students. I didn't know until recently
that the story was based on a real person.

A Few Good Women

When LouAnne Johnson got out of high school, she discovered she didn't much care for
college. She lasted forty-five days before dropping out and enlisting in the U.S. Navy.
There she flourished. She served eight years, and along the way she earned a degree in psychology. Then she decided to join the U.S. Marines, completed officer candidate school,
and served as a second lieutenant. But nine years into her military service, Johnson did
some soul-searching and decided to leave the service. She wanted something more.

For a while she worked for the *New York Times* in sales, where she earned a good
salary. But she didn't find it rewarding enough.

"I had been reading about kids graduating from school who couldn't read, couldn't
write and didn't have the basic literacy skills," she recalled. "I thought it was criminal,
if it was true." She moved to the West Coast, took a job as an executive assistant at
Xerox Corporation, and enrolled in college to earn her master's degree. Her desire was
to become a teacher. "I decided I would rather make $25,000 and do something that was
really important."[1]

The Class from Hell

When Johnson completed her degree, she took a position as an intern at Parkmont High
School in Belmont, California, a town south of San Francisco in San Mateo County. It
was a lot like the class depicted in the movie.

"What they [administrators] didn't say was that this veteran teacher had been driven
off by these kids," Johnson stated. "That first day they were just wild. They acted like I
wasn't there." She came back the next day with great resolve. She continued, "I told
them I was too young to retire and too mean to quit."[2]

She quickly developed strategies for connecting with the students. "I tried to use humor rather than threats," explained Johnson. "Sometimes I would get on my knees and say: 'Please don't make me beg. It's so unattractive.' You can't be a tough guy when you're smiling at the teacher."[3]

But more than anything else, her deep belief in her students won them over. A practice she developed for the first day of class—something she called her "card trick"—is typical of the kinds of things she did. She passed out index cards for students to supply name, address, phone number, and personal information. While they completed the cards, she walked the room with her roll sheet, glancing at their cards to see their names, which she secretly memorized.

As each teenager finished the information, she picked up each card and individually thanked each student. When she had all of the cards, she announced that the students were about to have their first test. The grumbling began, but she let them know that the test wasn't for them—it was for her. If she could name each student, she would win. If she missed even one name, every student would get an automatic A on the first test.

After she named every student (which she always succeeded in doing), many of the kids were impressed. And she told them, "I know your names because you are important people to me. When I look at you, I see you. I like you. And I care about you. That's why I'm here."[4]

PUTTING HER MONEY WHERE HER MOUTH IS

Johnson's attitude wasn't restricted to parlor tricks, such as the one she did learning students' names. She lived it out every day. Once when a student named Raul was in debt for one hundred dollars to a street tough, Johnson lent him the money. But it was on one condition. Raul, who was a sophomore, could pay her back only on the day he graduated.

Raul's journal revealed the impact that Johnson's actions made on him:

Last week, you told us to write in our journals about the nicest thing anybody ever did for us and I had to make something up because nobody never did nothing nice for me that I can remember before now. So I wrote you a lie . . . Anyway, what you did yesterday was the nicest thing and I think you did it because you think I am wonderful, honest, smart, and special! (That's what you always tell us anyway and I think you really believe it.) Anyway, I am going to work harder in school so I won't let you down because if you think I can make it then I can make it.[5]

Johnson believed in her students so much that they began to believe in themselves. Raul, whose father and mother had stopped going to school in third and second grades, hung in there and graduated. He was the first person in his family to earn a high school diploma.

"Our team held high expectations for our students," said Johnson, "too high, many people said. Don't ask for too much, they warned. Passing grades and graduation would be good enough. But we wanted more. We asked our students to come to school every single day, to stay away from drugs and alcohol, to change their bad habits, to complete every classroom and homework assignment, to resist the pressure to join gangs, to give up their bad attitudes and clean up their language. We asked for everything we could think of, and they gave us everything they had."[6]

"I think it's almost a political statement to be a teacher," Johnson explained. "What you're saying is that you believe in the children of this country and you're not giving up on them. It's almost like being a Peace Corps volunteer."[7] And that's why she wrote about her experience. "I wrote the book [My Posse Don't Do Homework] after working with at-risk teens because I was concerned about how easily adults give up on kids who have made mistakes. If we give up on them, they give up on themselves. BUT, if we believe they can overcome the challenges they face, they believe it, too."[8] In other words, Johnson is convinced that believing the best in people brings out the best in them.

You're a 10!

I embrace this principle with all of my heart. It's the reason I have taught people for more than thirty years. I am convinced that all people have potential. If people will only believe in themselves, they can reach their potential and become the individuals they were created to be. And here's how I think of it as I interact with people: I believe everyone I meet is a 10. That's why I call this the Number 10 Principle.

Do you believe that all people have potential? Why or why not?

_____

_____

_____

Back in 1983, I did a presentation at the Spokane Convention Center that has been broadcast often on Jim Dobson's *Focus on the Family* program. It probably best illustrates how I feel about people. It was called "Five Things I Know About People," and here is the essence of it:

1. Everybody Wants to Be Somebody

Author George M. Adams states, "There are high spots in all of our lives and most of them have come about through encouragement from someone else. I don't care how great, how famous or successful a man or woman may be, each hungers for applause." Don't you find that to be true? Everyone wants his life to matter. Everyone wants to feel significant. Don't you feel that way? Then you know it's true for everybody, even those who don't show it.

2. Nobody Cares How Much You Know Until He Knows How Much You Care

LouAnne Johnson worked with kids who had little interest in learning. The majority of students in their circumstances dropped out of school as soon as they could. She beat those odds by letting her students know that she cared about them—really cared. And once they understood that, they opened up to receive what she had to offer in the way of education. Too often we want to help people with what we know instead of caring for them because of who they are.

3. Everybody Needs Somebody

There isn't a person in the world who doesn't need other people. If we're honest, the issue often isn't *whether* we need others; the issue is, *How much* do we need others?

I recently received an email from my friend Steve Babby. It told the story of a kid named Fred, who played on a summer basketball league team coached by Corky Calhoun, a former college player from the University of Pennsylvania. Fred's team had the best players in the league, and it was obvious that they were destined to win. But Corky could see that Fred had serious problems with his confidence and self-image. Corky challenged players to help Fred believe in himself. So every time Fred scored a basket, they praised him mightily.

By the end of the season, two things happened. The team won the championship, and Fred believed he was the best player on the team, which he had become. Fred wasn't the same after that, but he never could have done it on his own. It took the help and belief of other people.

Who do you know that could use encouragement like Fred? How can you begin to encourage him or her?

_____

_____

_____

4. Anybody that Helps Somebody Influences Lots of Bodies

When LouAnne Johnson won Raul's heart, she got the rest of his "posse" with him. Raul was a tiny kid—ninety-five pounds at age seventeen (a result of eating beans and rice nearly every meal of his life). Since grammar school, he had spent his time with three friends who always considered him to be the clown of the group. However, once he started studying hard, his role among his friends changed. At first, they resented it, but soon they started to see him as an example. Before long, all of them were studying and trying to improve themselves.

By helping Raul, Johnson had helped all four. And that's the way it often turns out. When you help one person, it overflows into the lives of others.

How has the help you've given one person overflowed into the lives of others? How did that make you feel? What strategy can you use in helping others to maximize its impact?

_____

_____

_____

5. Somebody Today Will Rise Up and Become Somebody

When you believe in people—when you see each person as a 10—every day is a great day. Why? Because every morning brings a day in which someone's life can change. What a wonderful gift! LouAnne Johnson had no idea that her offer to lend a kid money would turn his life around when she got up that morning. But she looked at every day as an opportunity to make a difference. If you believe in people, each day can hold the same promise for you.

It's Better to Believe

Life holds that promise for me. I really believe in people and see the best in them. It is one of my greatest strengths. At times, it can also be a great weakness. I'm sometimes too trusting, and I desire to empower others before they're ready. Occasionally it gets me into trouble. But I'm willing to live with that risk because the rewards for others are so great. Our disappointment in a few people should not stop us from believing in people.

A Trusting Heart Is Emotionally Healthy

In his book *The Trusting Heart*, Dr. Redford Williams, director of the Behavioral Medicine Research Center at Duke University Medical Center, writes, "Those who have a trusting heart are more likely to remain healthy throughout most of their lives and to live long." He says that such a heart "believes in the basic goodness of humankind, that most people will be fair and kind in relationships with others." A soft heart is more likely to be a healthy one.

Do you agree that a soft heart is more likely to be a healthy one? Explain.

_____

_____

_____

We Behave in Light of Our Beliefs

If you don't like people or don't believe in them, you won't be able to fake it. The students in LouAnne Johnson's class responded to her because they could tell her affection for them was real. It wasn't an act. It was action rooted in her belief in people. If you desire to add value to people, then you need to value them first.

A Healthy Marriage Is Built on High Expectations

If you are married, the most important person for you to believe in is your spouse. At a Living Leadership conference in 2003, Marcus Buckingham, senior vice president of the Gallup Organization and co-author of *Now, Discover Your Strengths*, said that the number one sign of a healthy marriage is that spouses see each other more positively than other people do. And anytime a partner esteems his or her spouse lower than outsiders do, it's a sign that there is trouble in the relationship.

My experience as a pastor counseling people bears this out. When I saw couples during premarital counseling, each person thought the other could do no wrong. And when I saw couples who were contemplating divorce, each person thought the other could do no right.

Each of us has to be realistic about his or her spouse. Nobody's perfect, and no person can make another person happy. But if you're married and you don't believe in your spouse and support him or her 100 percent, then get some help because your relationship could be headed for trouble.

If you are married or in a relationship, what are some ways you can support your partner?

_____

_____

_____

Expressing Belief in People's Potential Encourages Them to Reach Their Potential

It's not enough just to believe in people, to think they are 10s. You need to express that belief. Philosopher-poet Johann Wolfgang von Goethe said, "Treat a man as he appears to be and you make him worse. But treat a man as if he already were what he potentially could be, and you make him what he should be."

APPLYING THE NUMBER 10 PRINCIPLE

1. What characteristics does a person display who desires to go it alone in life? Name some things that may cause that attitude. Why is it often difficult to help someone who has that mind-set? If you have that mind-set, in what way does it make it difficult for you to help others?

_____

_____

_____

2. In what ways—both positive and negative—does people's desire to be "somebody" show itself? In general, has your desire for recognition or significance driven you in a positive or negative direction? How do you think that colors your reaction to others' desire for attention? Has it made you supportive or resentful?

_____

_____

_____

3. Where do you find it easier to believe in people: at home or at work? Explain your answer. How do you desire to change? What positive steps could you take to change?

_____

_____

_____

4. Name some ways a person can *express* belief in others. How would you rate your practice of expressing belief in others: poor, average, or excellent? Why? Would your family and colleagues agree with you? Which of the means of expression that were named could you adopt and use to better express yourself?

_____

_____

_____

SUMMARY

Think about the people who have made a difference in your life: the teacher who made you believe you could achieve; the boss who gave you a chance to show that you could do it; the counselor who let you know you had what it takes to change and have a better life; the man or woman who loved you enough to say, "I do." Not only were they *there* at pivotal times, in many cases they probably *created* those pivotal times in your life.

In almost every instance where the impact was positive, the person believed in you. He or she probably saw something in you that perhaps you didn't even see in yourself. Wouldn't you like to be that person to others? If the answer is yes, then try to love others and see them as 10s. If you have a family, start with your spouse and your kids. And then broaden the circle from there. Believe the best in others, and you will bring out their best.

THE CONFRONTATION PRINCIPLE

CARING FOR PEOPLE SHOULD PRECEDE CONFRONTING PEOPLE

*Conflict is like cancer: early detection
increases the possibility of a healthy outcome.*

THE QUESTION I MUST ASK MYSELF:
DO I CARE ENOUGH
TO CONFRONT THE RIGHT WAY?

Years ago when I arrived at Skyline Church in San Diego, California, to become its senior pastor, I was following the founding pastor, Orval Butcher. When I first learned that he was retiring and the position would soon be open, some people advised me not to consider taking it. In the church world, it can be very tough following a founding pastor, especially one like Pastor Butcher who had served there for twenty-seven years and had done a wonderful job. Everybody loved Orval Butcher.

A Question of Loyalty

Like many leaders or executives who come into an organization from the outside, I soon found that not everyone was immediately on board with the change. Fortunately, because the people were very gracious and Pastor Butcher had been a good leader, most accepted me. I quickly settled in and began building relationships.

One Sunday a few months after I had arrived there, I noticed that Sally Johnson was there without her husband, Joe. They had always been active in the church and were consistent in attendance. And it occurred to me that I hadn't seen Joe in a couple of weeks. So I asked Sally how he was doing.

"Well, to be honest," she said, "he's having a difficult time with the changes here at church, and he didn't want to come."

I immediately called Joe and asked if he was willing to meet with me.

A few days later, Joe sat down with me in my office, and I said, "Joe, how are you doing? Sally tells me you're having a hard time with the transition."

"I guess you could say that," answered Joe. "I just miss Pastor Butcher."

"Joe," I said, "would you do something for me?"

"What?" Joe asked a little suspiciously.

"Tell me what you love about Pastor Butcher."

Joe looked surprised by the request, but he was happy to comply.

"Well," Joe began, "Pastor Butcher was always there for us. He married every one of our kids. He buried my mom and my dad. He did my brother's funeral, too." Joe went on to talk about how Orval Butcher had been at their side during the most important moments of their lives.

"It's no wonder that Pastor Butcher has such a special place in your heart," I said. Joe looked like he was fighting back tears. "Joe, Pastor Butcher should always be your favorite. And let me tell you something. I'll never be offended if he is *always* number one. I give you my permission for him to always be your favorite pastor." Joe's eyes sparkled, and a weight seemed to have lifted from his shoulders. "And if you ever have any love left over, just throw a little bit my way."

Joe was back at church the next Sunday, and he was his old self again. Every now and then, he would sneak up on me and give me a great big hug, saying, "Pastor, I have a little love left over this month." He did that until the day he died.

THE TRUTH ABOUT CONFLICT

My interaction with Joe Johnson turned out well, but as you can imagine, not all of my conflicts have ended so positively. Like anyone else, I've had my share of confrontations that ended poorly. But most of the time they went well, and I'll tell you why. I went into them with the mind-set of caring about the other person and trying to help him.

I could have pushed Joe Johnson. I could have drawn a line in the sand and said, "You follow me or else." That's the way a lot of leaders handle it when they come into an organization. That's one reason there is often high turnover when a department or organization has a new leader. Or I could have simply given up on Joe. I could have said, "He was part of the old guard. He obviously doesn't care for me, so why bother?" Instead, I acknowledged him and validated his feelings. It wasn't about competition. It would have been foolish to think that I could replace Orval Butcher in his heart. And it would have been inappropriate to try. It would be like a new stepparent saying bad things about a child's biological parent and trying to steal the child's affection.

I believe that we instinctively know some things about relationships to be true:

Conflict Is Unavoidable

Perhaps we ought to add conflict to death and taxes as one of the things we can count on in this life. The only way to avoid conflict is to isolate ourselves from all other people on the planet. Although if you've seen the movie *Castaway* with Tom Hanks where his character argues with a volleyball, you know that even people in isolation can find a way to create conflict.

Confrontation Is Difficult

Why is it difficult to confront? We fear being disliked, misunderstood, or rejected. We fear the unknown. We're not used to sharing our feelings. And we worry that we will just make things worse. Let's face it: few people have been taught healthy confrontation skills.

When faced with confronting someone, what is your greatest fear?

_____

_____

_____

How We Handle Conflict Determines Our Success in Tough Situations

How do you handle conflict in your relationships? Did you know that conflict always compounds when confrontation is not done quickly and correctly? That's why your approach matters. Here's a sampling of harmful strategies that I see people using when they deal with conflict:

- *Win at all costs.* It's like a shootout at the OK Corral. It's quick, brutal, and destructive.
- *Pretend it doesn't exist.* If you hear no evil, see no evil, and speak no evil, evil will not cease to exist.
- *Whine about it.* Winners aren't whiners and whiners aren't winners. Playing the victim doesn't cure conflict. It just irritates everybody.
- *Keep score.* People who keep a record of wrongs can't ever start over fresh. And nobody can ever get "even."
- *Pull rank.* Using position never really resolves conflict. It merely postpones it.
- *White flag it.* Quitting is a permanent solution to a temporary problem.

None of these approaches will give the help a person needs to resolve conflict in a healthy way.

A Road Map for Healthy Confrontation

Conflict resolution isn't complicated. Intellectually it's simple. But emotionally it can be difficult. It requires honesty, humility, and dedication to the relationship. Here is a six-step plan to help you tackle the task of confrontation:

1. Confront a Person Only If You Care for that Person

In rare instances people must confront someone they don't care about, such as in legal trials or when abuse has occurred. But these are not typical relational conflicts. In nearly all relational situations, it is most productive to go into a confrontation keeping the other person's interests in mind.

In the past when you attempted to resolve conflict with another person, what has been your goal? Sympathy? Quick relief? Victory at all costs? Next time try to go into it with the goal of making it a win for both parties. And if you attempt to ensure that the other person wins first, then you know you have the most beneficial perspective.

Is there someone you need to confront? Explain why this person is important to you.

_____

_____

_____

2. Meet Together ASAP

Whenever conflict arises, we are tempted to avoid it, procrastinate dealing with it, or ask someone else to resolve it for us. But the truth is that anytime you let conflict go—for whatever reason—it only gets worse. If people are put in a position to start speculating about another person's motives or to figure out what might have really happened, they often think the worst. Putting off confrontation only allows the situation to fester.

3. First Seek Understanding, Not Necessarily Agreement

A significant hindrance to positive conflict resolution is having too many preconceived notions going into a confrontation. There's a saying that the person who gives an opinion before he understands is human, but the person who gives a judgment before he understands is a fool.

How do you seek understanding when in conflict with another person?

_____

_____

_____

4. Outline the Issue

When it's your turn to speak and to make yourself understood, it's important that you take a positive approach. Here's what I suggest:

- *Describe your perceptions.* In the beginning, stay away from conclusions and/or statements about the other person's motives. Just tell what you think you see, and describe the problem you think it's causing.

- *Tell how this makes you feel.* If the other person's actions make you angry or frustrated or sad, express it clearly and without accusation.

- *Explain why this is important to you.* Many times when a person finds out that something is a priority to you, this is enough to make him want to change.

Engaging in this process without emotional heat or bitterness is essential. You don't have to turn off your emotions; you just need to make sure you don't verbally assault the person you're confronting.

5. Encourage a Response

Never confront others without letting them respond. If you care about people, you will want to listen. Besides, as politician Dean Rusk stated, "One of the best ways to persuade others is with your ears—by listening to them."

Sometimes simply having the discussion helps you to realize that your perceptions were wrong. I know that's happened to me. It's very humbling when I realize *I* am the problem. Other times you discover that you need to take extenuating circumstances into account. Encouraging a response helps you better understand the problem.

It also gives the other person a chance to process emotionally. Most of the time when you confront people, they will have an emotional reaction. They may be shocked or get angry or feel guilty. They may want to share those feelings with you, or they may not. But no matter what, you should encourage them to give you a genuine response.

Why? Because if they don't have their say, they won't be able to move toward a resolution to the problem. They will be so focused on their response that they can't hear anything else.

When confronting people, I've discovered the following:

50 percent of the time people don't realize there is a problem.

30 percent of them realized there was a problem, but didn't know how to solve it.

20 percent realized there was a problem, but didn't want to solve it.

The bad news is that one out of five people doesn't want to seek positive resolution. The good news is that 80 percent of the time there is great potential to solve the conflict.

6. Agree to an Action Plan

Most people hate confrontation, but they love resolution. And the only way to achieve resolution is to take positive action. By developing and agreeing to an action plan, you place the focus on the future, not on the problems of the past. If the person you're confronting wants to change, he will gravitate toward the possibility of making things better.

A good action plan should include these points:

a) Clear identification of the issue

b) Agreement to solve the issue

c) Concrete steps that demonstrate the issue has been solved

d) An accountability structure, such as a timeline and responsible person

e) A deadline for completion

f) A commitment by both parties to put the issue in the past once resolved

If your confrontation is formal, such as in a work setting, then put the action plan in writing. Then you can always go back to that document if resolution doesn't go as planned.

Successful confrontation usually changes both people, not just one. Did you know that people begin to have similar opinions of one another over time? Some people call this the reciprocity rule. Positive change is the first measure of success when resolving conflict through confrontation. The second is the ongoing growth of the relationship.

Anytime you truly do resolve conflict in a relationship, it doesn't hurt the relationship; rather, it actually strengthens the bond between the people.

APPLYING THE CONFRONTATION PRINCIPLE

1. What happens when a confrontation doesn't go well? Have you been involved in a confrontation that went badly? Were you the confronter or the one being confronted? Explain what went wrong. What did it do to the relationship?

_____

_____

_____

2. Would you say that most people have the other person's best interests at heart during a confrontation? What often motivates people to confront others? How about your motivations? Are they usually altruistic or self-defensive?

_____

_____

_____

3. Consider the various ways people often react to potential conflict: *Win at all costs. Walk away from it. Pretend it doesn't exist. Whine about it. Keep score. Pull rank. White flag it.* In the past, which approach have you been most likely to take? Why? How would you like to handle conflict in the future? What steps must you take to improve in this area?

_____

_____

_____

4. What happens when the person initiating the confrontation becomes overly emotional? How about when he doesn't? What can one do to remain emotionally even-tempered during a confrontation?

_____

_____

_____

5. What often happens when no clear action plan has been created as part of a confrontation? Do you find it difficult to create such plans? What are some of the common roadblocks? What happens if the other person doesn't wish to participate? How do you come to resolution and closure in such cases?

_____

_____

_____

SUMMARY

Bo Schembechler, the former head football coach of the University of Michigan, said, "Deep down, your players must know you care about them. This is the most important thing. I could never get away with what I do if the players felt I didn't care. They know, in the long run, I'm in their corner." When you get ready to confront someone, he should have that same kind of sense from you. Abraham Lincoln summed it up when he said, "If you would win a man to your cause, first convince him that you are his sincere friend . . . Assume to dictate to his judgment, or to command his action, or to mark him as one to be shunned and despised, and he will retreat within himself . . . you shall no more be able to pierce him than to penetrate the hard shell of a tortoise with a rye straw."

THE TRUST QUESTION
CAN WE BUILD MUTUAL TRUST?

The glory of friendship is not the outstretched hand,
not the kindly smile, nor the joy of companionship; it is the spiritual
inspiration that comes to one when you discover that someone else
believes in you and is willing to trust you with a friendship.

—RALPH WALDO EMERSON

Why do many relationships fall apart? Some marriages that begin with great passion come to a bitter end. Friendships that people hope will last for a lifetime falter and die. Business partnerships that began with promise come to a disastrous conclusion. The reasons for such breakdowns are many, but the cause that outweighs all others is broken trust.

How do you define trust? *Webster's New World Dictionary*, third edition, calls *trust* a "firm belief or confidence in the honesty, integrity, reliability, justice, etc. of another person." Kevin Myers says, "You may not know what trust is, but you know what it isn't." If people lie to you, steal from you, or physically harm you, then you know you can't trust them. That's obvious. But are there other ways that a person can break trust? Are there things people can do to make a relationship unworthy of trust? For that matter, what kind of person must *you* be in a relationship in order to be worthy of another person's trust?

These questions are at the heart of the next five chapters. And the People Principles contained in them will help you answer the question, "Can we build mutual trust?"

The Bedrock Principle: Trust is the foundation of any relationship.

The Situation Principle: Never let the situation mean more than the relationship.

The Bob Principle: When Bob has a problem with everyone, Bob is usually the problem.

The Approachability Principle: Being at ease with ourselves helps others be at ease with us.

The Foxhole Principle: When preparing for battle, dig a hole big enough for a friend.

THE BEDROCK PRINCIPLE

Trust Is the Foundation
of Any Relationship

It is a greater compliment to be trusted than to be loved.

—George MacDonald

THE QUESTION I MUST ASK MYSELF:
AM I A TRUSTWORTHY PERSON?

He was a promising young journalist. He was energetic and hardworking. The principal of his high school remembered, "He was always into the newspaper business, even here. He had a wonderful, positive persistence about him that we all admired."[1] At the University of Maryland where he went to school, he was remembered as a productive and talented writer. That reputation won him a ten-week summer internship at the top newspaper in the country: the *New York Times*. There he was said to have done very well, having written nineteen articles and helped with many others.

That was in 1998. The next summer he returned to the *Times* for a job and was soon promoted to intermediate reporter. He did the kind of work an entry-level reporter is assigned, and he was successful, though he was warned about being too sloppy in his work. In January 2001, Jayson Blair became a full-time reporter.

Despite his progress, not everything was going smoothly with Blair. His editors continued to admonish him for sloppy work. Jonathan Landman, the paper's metropolitan editor, told Blair his correction rate was "extraordinarily high by the standards of the paper."[2] That didn't set well with the editor. As he told his staff in an email, "Accuracy is all we have. It's what we are and what we sell."[3] Because of Blair's talent and potential, editors checked up on him frequently and worked with him to help him improve his accuracy in reporting. Eventually he was transferred to the sports department.

Somehow along the way, he was rerouted from sports to the national desk and then sent to help report on the sniper case in Virginia. Reporting on national stories, he flourished and made a name for himself. He broke a huge story on the sniper case. He reported on the family of POW Jessica Lynch, who was taken prisoner in Iraq. And he wrote many other high-profile stories.

THE REST OF THE STORY

But then Jayson Blair got into trouble. Big trouble. Someone noticed that parts of a story he submitted from southern Texas about the mother of a slain American soldier were remarkably similar to a story by another reporter written several days before his. An editor from the *San Antonio Express-News*, who had published the original story, emailed the editors at the *Times* to alert them to the problem. That prompted the paper to look more closely at Blair's past work.

The *Times* staff found that one hundred of the more than six hundred articles Blair wrote for the *Times* had problems or needed significant corrections.[4] And nearly half of the articles he wrote for national reporting assignments had problems. But Blair was guilty of more than sloppy reporting. Former *New York Times* editor Howell Raines says an investigation revealed a "pathological pattern of misrepresentation, fabricating and deceiving."[5] Blair had lied to his bosses, pretending to go on assignment and then filing false "firsthand" stories. He had fabricated parts of stories using photos and other news sources. And he had plagiarized other reporters' work. He even filed false expense reports to try to cover his tracks.

When the story broke, its impact was huge. The credibility of the *New York Times* was at stake. Representatives at the *Times* called it a "huge black eye" and the "low point" in the paper's 152-year history.[6] *Times* writers commented, "Although the deceit of one *Times* reporter does not impugn the work of 375 others, experts and teachers of journalism say that the *Times* must repair the damage done to the public trust."[7]

Blair resigned in the wake of the revelations. His former bosses, colleagues, and friends no longer trusted him, and many expressed anger at him for his betrayal.[8] The reporter whose south Texas story he plagiarized—Macarena Hernandez, who ironically had served as a *New York Times* intern with Blair—says of him, "His story is that of a guy who disrespected his profession, cheated his readers, deceived his editors and stole from his peers. Period. Any other way of looking at it lets Jayson Blair off the hook."[9]

What was Blair doing all those times he was supposed to be on assignment? According to *New York Times* reporters, he was hiding out in his Brooklyn apartment, fabricating stories, and working on a book proposal on the sniper story. After the news of his deception broke, he changed tacks and wrote instead about his exploits at the *New York Times*. One writer who reviewed the resulting book, titled *Burning Down My Master's House*, called Blair a "world-class Pinocchio" and a "confessed serial liar."[10] The book's publisher evidently expected it to do well, having ordered a first printing of 250,000 copies. But *Time* magazine reported that after being available for nine days, it sold only 1,400 copies.[11] I guess that means nobody believed what Jayson Blair had to say.

Think of a person you don't trust and a person you completely trust. Why do you trust the one person and not the other?

_____

_____

_____

TRUST ME ON THIS

It is impossible to overestimate the importance of truth when it comes to trust. The article in the *New York Times* that outlined Blair's deceptions included the following statements: "Every newspaper, like every bank and every police department, trusts its employees to uphold central principles, and the inquiry found that Mr. Blair repeatedly violated the cardinal tenet of journalism, which is simply truth."[12]

If you boil relationships down to the most important element, it's always going to be trust—not leadership, value, partnership, or anything else. If you don't have trust, your relationship is in trouble. Here's why:

Trust Is the Foundation of Any Relationship

In *The 21 Irrefutable Laws of Leadership*, I wrote about the Law of Solid Ground: "Trust is the foundation of leadership."[13] In his book *On Becoming a Leader*, Warren Bennis says, "Integrity is the basis of trust, which is not so much an ingredient of leadership as it is a product. It is the one quality that cannot be acquired, but must be earned. It is given by coworkers and followers, and without it, the leader can't function."

That can be said not only of leaders and followers, but also of all relationships. Developing trust is like constructing a building. It takes time, and it must be done one piece at a time. As in construction, it's much quicker and easier to tear something down than it is to build it up. But if the foundation is strong, there is a good chance that what is built upon it will stand.

How does trust factor into your relationships with others?

_____

_____

_____

Trust Is the Frame of Any Relationship

A relationship can also be described as being like a painting. Trust is like the frame that surrounds it—and holds it together. It provides a context in which to view the work of art. Trust defines its boundaries. And trust secures it to the wall so that it can be enjoyed. Trust provides emotional structure.

EARNING OTHERS' TRUST

Psychologist and consultant Jack R. Gibb observed, "trust is the result of a risk successfully survived." What a wonderful description! When others trust us, they truly take a risk. But with each successive time people put their trust in us and we don't let them down, we reduce that risk and build the relationship. If you desire to build your trustworthiness—and as a result, your relationships—remember these three truths about trust:

1. Trust Begins with Yourself

Shakespeare wrote, "This above all: To thine own self be true, and it must follow, as the night the day, thou canst not then be false to any man." If you are not honest with yourself, you will not be capable of honesty with others. Self-deception is the enemy of relationships. It also undermines personal growth. If a person does not admit his shortcomings, he cannot improve them.

It all goes back to the Mirror Principle. The first person we must examine is ourself. Take a good look at yourself. Are you honest with yourself about how you live your life? Is your character solid? Does your yes mean yes and your no mean no? Do you follow through with your commitments? Don't ask others to put their confidence in you if you believe you may betray it. Work on your character first, then your relationships.

2. Trust Cannot Be Compartmentalized

Cheryl Biehl, wife of friend and author Bobb Biehl, says, "One of the realities of life is that if you can't trust a person at all points, you can't truly trust him or her at any point." I believe that to be true. Unfortunately I think many people today try to compartmentalize their lives. They believe that they can cut corners or compromise their values in one area of life and it won't affect another area. But character doesn't work that way. And neither does trust.

In 2003, I wrote a book called *There's No Such Thing as "Business" Ethics*. The premise is that you can't have one set of ethics for your business life and another for your personal life.

Character doesn't work that way. If someone asks you to help him in a lie, don't believe that he will avoid lying to you whenever it's convenient. What a person will do *with* you, he'll also do *to* you. An individual's character eventually bleeds into every aspect of his life.

Do you have the same ethical standards for work as you have for home? Explain.

_____

_____

_____

3. Trust Works Like a Bank Account

Mike Abrashoff, author of *It's Your Ship*, states, "Trust is like a bank account—you have got to keep making deposits if you want it to grow. On occasion, things will go wrong, and you will have to make a withdrawal. Meanwhile, it is sitting in the bank earning interest."[14]

Mike learned that from his years as a naval officer. I learned the same thing as a pastor. For years at leadership conferences, I taught the idea of having "change" in your pocket relationally. When you first begin a relationship with someone, you start fresh with that person. If the person is trusting and generous, you may begin with a little bit of change. If he is suspicious or hurting, you probably begin with none. Each time you do something to build trust, you put relational change in your pocket. Each time you do something negative, you spend some of that change. Do enough negative things—due to lack of character or competence—and you're bankrupt. And that spells the end of the relationship.

This dynamic works in every area of your life. If you spend all of your change with your colleagues at work, they no longer willingly work with you. If you spend all of your change with your boss, you end up looking for another job. If you spend all of your change with your friends, you spend a lot of time alone. If you spend all of your change with your spouse, you end up in divorce court.

If this is a new concept to you, then you need to ask yourself some questions at the end of every day:

- *Am I making deposits?* Think about your most important relationships. Are you exhibiting trustworthy behavior that's putting relational "money in the bank"?

- *Am I making withdrawals?* Have you undermined trust in any of those important relationships? If so, you need to try to make things right. Don't wait another minute to take the appropriate action by doing the following:

1. Apologize.
2. Ask yourself why you broke trust.
3. Correct the issue in your life.
4. Recognize that it takes longer to restore trust than to lose it.
5. Remember, trust is restored by deeds, not just words.

Doing these things won't earn you new change, but it may stop you from losing more. And you just might save the relationship.

- *Am I compounding my trust?* Mike Krzyzewski, head basketball coach at Duke University, offers this advice: "If you set up an atmosphere of communication and trust, it becomes a tradition. Older team members will establish your credibility with newer ones. Even if they don't like everything about you, they'll still say, 'He's trustworthy, committed to us as a team.'" You can, as Mike Abrashoff says, develop so much trust that it actually builds without additional deposits. But it takes time and incredible consistency.

WHAT IF YOU'RE RELUCTANT TO TRUST OTHERS?

I've given a lot of my attention in this chapter to the concept of *being* a trustworthy person. But I recognize that some trustworthy people have a difficult time trusting others. Perhaps people have broken trust with you. If so, attempt to take these three steps:

1. *Forgive them.* Because you are in the right, you have power over the other persons. Please don't abuse that power.

2. *Explain that the violation must never happen again.* Forgiving others doesn't mean allowing them to continue hurting you.

3. *Remember their better moments.* We all have our highs and lows. It takes maturity to treat people according to their best qualities.

Is there someone in your life whom you need to forgive? If so, start working on it now. Describe the offense. Now, write out your forgiveness of the person. Follow up and forgive the individual personally.

_____

_____

_____

There is great relief in forgiving others. If you desire to forgive and begin trusting again, then take to heart these words of Henry L. Simpson, former U.S. Secretary of State: "The chief lesson I have learned in a long life is that the only way you can make a man trustworthy is by trusting him; and the surest way to make him untrustworthy is to distrust him and show your distrust." As I already mentioned, trusting others is a risk, but it's a risk worth taking. Without trust, you cannot build healthy, lasting relationships.

Take the plunge. I'm not saying you will never get hurt. You might. But I can say this. You'll never experience the joy that comes only from relationships unless you're willing to give trust a try.

APPLYING THE FOUNDATION PRINCIPLE

1. How does being reluctant to trust others affect someone's ability to connect? What can someone who doesn't easily trust others do to change that natural reluctance?

_____

_____

_____

2. What happens to a relationship when one person exhibits untrustworthiness? Describe how relationships break down over time. Is a relationship ever beyond hope? If not, explain why. If so, describe how one would know. Is your answer the same for relationships in every area of life: with friends, colleagues, a spouse, or children?

_____

_____

_____

3. Think about someone with whom you have spent a lot of your relational change. Describe some things you did that damaged the relationship. What can you do to rebuild trust and "bank" some change? What is currently preventing you from doing these things?

_____

_____

_____

4. Broken trust is not always a character issue. Sometimes it comes from lack of competence or lack of communication. Which issues erode trust most quickly? From which of these issues can a relationship recover more quickly? Explain.

_____

_____

_____

5. What happens when someone's inner circle contains untrustworthy people? How does that affect his ability to achieve? How does that affect his character? How hard is it to change the kinds of people with whom one associates? What steps can one take to create a new inner circle?

_____

_____

_____

Summary

Trust is the height of any relationship. When two people trust each other completely, the relationship can grow to a level of friendship that is as rewarding as anything in life. It reaches the highest heights. Writer and chaplain to Queen Victoria, Charles Kingsley, said, "A blessed thing it is for any man or woman to have a friend, one human soul whom we can trust utterly, who knows the best and worst of us, and who loves us in spite of all our faults."

THE SITUATION PRINCIPLE

NEVER LET THE SITUATION
MEAN MORE THAN THE RELATIONSHIP

*It is more rewarding to resolve a situation
than to dissolve a relationship.*

THE QUESTION I MUST ASK MYSELF:
DO I SOMETIMES PUT SITUATIONS
AHEAD OF MY RELATIONSHIPS?

W hat would you do if you had the opportunity of a lifetime to fulfill your dreams, to rise up and take your place among the elite in your profession, to become a champion? And what if only one person stood between you and your goal? Would you make the best of the situation? Would you seize the moment? What if the one person in your way was your sister?

SISTER ACT

That's the situation Serena Williams faced. If you're a tennis fan, you know who I'm talking about. But even if you don't follow tennis, you have probably still heard of the Williams sisters or seen sports shoe commercials that feature them.

Venus and Serena Williams were tennis prodigies. Their father, Richard, says that when he saw the televised image of a women's tennis champion at the 1978 French Open receiving a large check, he decided that if he and his wife had any more children, they would become pro tennis players. Venus was born in 1980 and Serena in 1981. When Venus was four, Richard Williams began to teach her the game in a park in Compton, California. A year later Serena joined their sessions.

The girls showed promise early and dominated everywhere they played. In 1991, Venus was ranked number one among twelve-and-under girls in highly competitive Southern California, and Serena was ranked number one in the ten-and-under division. But instead of keeping them in junior tennis, which was considered the normal route to the pros, Richard pulled them out of it, moved the family to Florida, and enrolled the girls in a top tennis academy, where they trained for four years.

In 1994, Venus became eligible to turn pro, and Richard put her in her first competition. She won her first match, but lost her second to the number two-ranked woman in the world. When reporters asked Venus how the loss compared to previous defeats, the teenager explained that she didn't know—because she had never lost a match before! The next year Reebok signed Venus to a multimillion-dollar endorsement deal. By the end of 1997, she was ranked sixty-fourth in the world. Meanwhile, Serena was also making a name for herself. At age sixteen, she finished just outside the top one hundred.

Growing up, the girls had trained together, practiced together, and played together. And the older Venus always had the upper hand. But they had never played against each other in a professional tournament. Then in 1998, the inevitable happened. The two young women faced each other in the second round of the Australian Open. And as expected, Venus won.

"It wasn't fun eliminating my little sister, but I have to be tough," Venus said after defeating Serena. "After the match, I said, 'I'm sorry I had to take you out.' Since I'm older, I have the feeling I should win."[1]

The Williams sisters continued to live and train together. They played doubles together and won. And when they met in the finals of the Lipton Championships in March 1999, it was a big deal. It was the first time two sisters had competed against each other in a pro women's tennis title since the Watson sisters at Wimbledon in 1884. Venus said, "The way we were playing, it was inevitable we'd meet in the final. And it's inevitable we'll meet again."[2] And once again, Venus won.

QUEST FOR THE BEST

But that year Serena got a taste of major success when she won the U.S. Open—it was the first time either sister had won a Grand Slam event. She was ready to go to a new level. Serena said, "I'm tired of losing to people I should beat. Whatever my potential is, I want to reach it—now. And if I do, I see Venus as my biggest competition."[3]

Then in October 1999, less than a month after her eighteenth birthday, Serena finally did it. She defeated her sister for the first time, winning the Grand Slam Cup in Munich. She went on to defeat Venus many more times. In 2002, Serena became the number one-ranked player in the world, and in 2003, she signed the biggest endorsement contract ever for a female athlete: $40 million with Nike.

And what did all this competition do to their relationship? Did they develop bad blood and come to hate each other? The answer is no. Just as they had since they were kids, they remained best friends. They continued to room together on tour. And when Serena skipped the Australian Open in 2004, Venus talked about how much she missed Serena.

"Family comes first, no matter how many times we play each other," says Serena. "Nothing will come between me and my sister."[4] Not fame, not fortune, not professional rank. They don't let any situation mean more than their relationship.

Do You?

Venus and Serena didn't choose to be sisters. Most of us don't get to choose who's family. But we *do* choose how we *treat* our family. We choose whether we nurture or neglect our family relationships. And let's face it: every family has someone who stretches relationships. How we treat that person is still our choice.

Describe a situation where you were competing with a friend or family member. How did you handle it?

_____

_____

_____

Many people expect relationships to be smooth sailing. That's really very naive. Just think about the way wedding vows are written. Typically they read something like this:

I take you to be my wedded wife, to have and to hold, from this day forward, for better or worse, for richer or poorer, in joy and sorrow, in sickness and in health, to love and to cherish, till death do us part, and hereto I pledge you my faithfulness.

Marriage vows assume that life is difficult and situations will occur that can cause separation: sorrow, poverty, sickness, and challenging times. The question is, When the tough times come, what will be more important to us: the situation or the relationship?

Take a moment to think about how your relationships usually work out. Now look at the following lists and circle the word on each line that best describes them:

Volatile	or	Steady
Deceitful	or	Open
Selfish	or	Mature
Draining	or	Refreshing
Insecure	or	Secure
Manipulating	or	Accepting
Conditional	or	Unconditional
Breaking	or	Bonding

The column on the left describes interaction where the relationship fluctuates with the situation. The column on the right describes interaction where the relationship is rock solid regardless of the situation.

MAKE THE DECISION FIRST

In *Today Matters*, I assert that successful people make right decisions early and manage those decisions daily. That's true when it comes to values, priorities, finances, faith, health—and especially relationships. Keeping a relationship strong is a decision. One reason the divorce rate is so high is that many people go into marriage without a firm commitment on the front end of the relationship to never let some situation mean more than the relationship.

Having said that, let me clarify. There are some life-or-death situations where the relationship becomes secondary. When a partner is being abusive, the other person needs to be concerned for his or her safety. But abuse is not involved in most situations where there is a relational breakdown. When some people find themselves in a situation where the relationship requires hard work, they must make personal sacrifices, or they simply don't feel "happy" enough, they bail out.

Other people violate the Situation Principle in other ways. They may not abandon the relationship. Instead, they stay around and damage it. Once again, they pay more attention to the situation than to the relationship. I have been guilty of this. As a parent of teenagers, I sometimes let the situation become too important to me, and as a result, my insensitivity to my children put a strain on our relationship. I also violated the Situation Principle in my marriage. I've already told you about how I won arguments but hurt my wife, Margaret, during our early years of marriage. And I've also let circumstances cloud my judgment as a leader, and as a result, I hurt my relationship with some of the people I led.

Anytime a person puts the situation ahead of the relationship, it happens for one reason: loss of perspective. That was true when I made mistakes with my family. It was the case as a leader. It will be the case for you if you violate the Situation Principle. People are always more important than mere things. Our property, our position or power, and our agenda are transitory.

How Can I Keep the Situation in Proper Perspective?

To keep your perspective and prevent you from allowing the situation to become more important than the relationship, you can ask yourself several questions. I suggest you start with these five:

1. Do I See the Big Picture—or Just the Bad Picture?

Whenever we experience a rough time in a relationship, we need to remind ourselves of why that relationship is significant to us in the first place. When a child comes home with a bad grade, when a spouse forgets to do something really important to us, or when a good friend lets us down, we may feel angry or disappointed. But what is that in the big scheme of things? What would you trade for your children? Your spouse? Your closest friends? Nothing is more important.

Think about your last disagreement. What was the Big Picture?

_____

_____

_____

2. Do I Communicate the Big Picture Along with the Bad One?

When I was a kid, my parents were marvelous at communicating the big picture to me, even as I was creating a bad one that required correction and discipline. They might spank or punish me when I deserved it, but they always told me they loved me. And when I was old enough to understand, they often explained the reasons behind their actions. I didn't always appreciate it at the time, but I realized later in life that it made me very secure in my relationship with them. Thanks to their perspective, I never lost sight of the big picture, no matter how bad I had been.

How do you communicate the Big Picture when correcting someone on your team?

_____

_____

_____

3. Is This a One-Time Situation or an Oft-Repeated One?

There is a big difference between a situation that occurs once and one that occurs again and again. Both affect the relationship, and both require commitment. However, a recurring issue will need the commitment from all parties involved to sustain the relationship and ultimately change the situation.

For example, if one member of a married couple makes a one-time mistake that hurts them financially, it's relatively easy to overcome it and sustain the relationship. But if one person continually blows the budget and puts the couple into deeper and deeper debt, only with a commitment from both of them—to sustain the relationship and to change their actions—will their relationship survive.

4. Do I Make Too Many Situations a Life-or-Death Issue?

Dean Smith, the former head basketball coach at North Carolina, observed, "If you make every game a life-and-death proposition . . . you'll be dead a lot." In other words, we need to pick our battles.

If you are, or have been, the parent of teenagers, you know from experience that this is true. If you make every issue something worth fighting about, you'll be fighting your children so much that you alienate them.

How do you know if you're making too many situations life-or-death issues? Answer these questions:

How often are you tense and upset?

_____

How often do you raise your voice when talking to others?

_____

How frequently are you battling for your personal rights or for what's right?

_____

If these issues occur day after day, your perspective may be off. Being in a constant state of agitation is not a healthy way to live, nor does it develop and maintain healthy relationships.

5. Do I Show My Unconditional Love During the Difficult Situations?

At some point, everyone faces difficult situations in close relationships. But not everyone handles those situations well. If you are able to communicate your love to those closest to you in the midst of pain or difficulty, you greatly increase the stability of the relationship.

APPLYING THE SITUATION PRINCIPLE

1. What pressures of life often cause people to place relationships as a lower priority than they should? How prone are you to allowing pressures to damage your relationships? What can you change to break unhealthy patterns?

_____

_____

_____

2. Under what circumstance does a relationship legitimately become less important than the situation? What can happen if one does not reprioritize in such situations?

_____

_____

_____

3. Have you ever known someone who made every little thing seem like a life-and-death situation? If so, what was the result? What was it like trying to develop a good relationship with him or her? Is it possible to sustain a healthy relationship with such a person? Explain.

_____

_____

_____

4. Think about an important relationship in which you allowed a situation to sway you to act badly. What happened as a result? Have you been able to repair the relationship? Have you apologized? What could you do now to improve or restore that relationship?

_____

_____

_____

5. Your relationships with your immediate family members are the most important ones in your life. What do those relationships mean to you? (If you've never expressed those ideas and feelings in writing, consider doing it now.) How can you use those thoughts to maintain the right perspective the next time you face a tough situation?

_____

_____

_____

Summary

My friend Tim Elmore told me the story of a girl named Deanna, a good high school student who usually earned high grades. As a college prep student, she enrolled in a chemistry class and worked hard. But for some reason, the subject just never clicked. And for the first time in her life, she failed a class.

Fortunately Deanna had an encouraging teacher. He believed in her and knew her poor performance was unusual. He was sure that she would succeed in college, but it bothered him to put an F on her report card. So what did he do? He couldn't in good conscience give her a passing grade. So in the margin next to the F, he wrote, "We cannot all be chemists—but, oh, how we would all love to be Deannas."

Make a decision to put your relationships ahead of the circumstances of life. If you do, you will develop deeper trust in your relationships, and they will go to a whole new level.

THE BOB PRINCIPLE

WHEN BOB HAS A PROBLEM WITH EVERYONE, BOB IS USUALLY THE PROBLEM

All seems infected that the infected spy,
As all looks yellow to the jaundiced eye.

—ALEXANDER POPE

THE QUESTION I MUST ASK MYSELF:
AM I BOB?

O n June 23, 1988, Billy Martin was fired as manager of major-league baseball's
New York Yankees. Baseball managers lose their jobs all the time, so that may
not sound like news. What was different was that Martin was being fired from
his job as Yankees manager for the fifth time!

NEW YORK, WE HAVE A PROBLEM

Have you ever known a person who had problems follow him wherever he went? That
seemed to be the case with Billy Martin. When he got called up to the Yankees in 1950
as a second baseman, he was joining one of the best teams of all time. And Martin, only
a .257 career hitter, held his own. He performed especially well during World Series
games and was named the Series' MVP in 1953. While he was with the Yankees as a
player (1950–57), the only year they did not win the pennant was 1954, the year Martin
was in the Army.

But despite his success, Martin's life was never smooth sailing. The problem was that
he often seemed to have a hard time getting along with people. The reason he left the
Yankees after seven seasons is that he was traded following a big fight in a nightclub
involving other Yankees players. It wasn't his first fight, nor would it be his last.

After Martin left the Yankees, he played for six other teams in four years: the
Athletics, Tigers, Indians, Reds, Braves, and Twins. He retired in 1961 and went on to
coach. In 1969 he became a manager. But everywhere he went, trouble followed. He was
legendary for the fistfights he started. The first one of note occurred in 1952, but there
are too many of them to list. Tobias Seamon of *The Morning News* summarizes Martin
this way:

The fights and insobriety [from his playing days] continued into Martin's managerial career.
In 1969 during his tenure as manager of the Minnesota Twins, he beat up his star pitcher
Dave Boswell and was fired. In 1974 with the Texas Rangers, he popped the team's 64-year-
old traveling secretary in a fight over a proposed club for the team's wives. Hired back as
manager of the Yankees in 1977, he took the team to a world title, but was, at one point,

seen battling with Reggie Jackson in the dugout during a nationally televised game, and was again relieved of his position. In 1979—again managing in Minnesota—he clobbered a marshmallow salesman.

The early eighties were the usual for Martin. Hired, fired, and rehired again by the Yankees, Martin drank and brawled his way out of every job he ever had. His teams almost always won, but the price of living with Martin was too much. Yankee star Ron Guidry said of the manager, "If you approach Billy Martin right, he's okay. I avoid him altogether."[1]

Martin was continually ejected from games and often suspended for his treatment of umpires. And he didn't get along with the owners of the teams that employed him either. (He once demanded a five-year contract extension; instead he received a pink slip.) Pulitzer Prize–winning sports columnist Jim Murray said of Martin, "Some people have a chip on their shoulder. Billy has a whole lumberyard."[2]

HE LOOKS LIKE A BOB TO ME

Billy Martin is the perfect example of what I call the Bob Principle. It's a relational truth I discovered years ago: if Bob has problems with Bill, and Bob has problems with Fred, and Bob has problems with Sue, and Bob has problems with Jane, and Bob has problems with Sam, then Bob is usually the problem.

Billy Martin seemed to have problems with nearly everyone. He was involved in more fights than some professional boxers! Yet he never indicated that he saw a problem with how he conducted himself. Martin said, "I believe if God had ever managed, he would have been very aggressive, the way I manage."[3] And why did he think he was fired from so many teams? He explained, "I get fired because I'm not a yes-man. The world's full of yes-men."[4]

Not every Bob gets into fistfights the way Billy Martin did. (Nor does every Bob get fired five times from the same job!) So how do you know a Bob when you see him? Look for the following four characteristics:

1. Bob Is a Problem Carrier

The Bobs of the world carry around problems, and those problems affect others. I first became aware of this truth only a few years into my professional career. At a monthly board meeting, a board member would bring up an issue, saying that a member of the congregation was having a problem with something I was doing. Immediately three or four other board members would say that they had heard the same kinds of complaints.

My first thought was to examine my actions. After reflecting, I still believed what I was doing was right, but I felt that if so many people had problems with it, I wondered if I needed to give it more consideration.

After this kind of thing happened several times, I made a decision. I talked to the board members, and we all agreed: if someone on the board heard a complaint, he needed to disclose who had made it.

The next time we met, sure enough one of the board members brought up a complaint he had heard. Several other board members confirmed that they had heard it, too. When the first board member revealed the name of the person who complained, the others said, "That's the same person who complained to me."

I felt like I was in the same situation as the old farmer who went to a restaurant owner to find out if he wanted to buy a million frog legs. When the proprietor asked where he could find so many frogs, the farmer replied, "I've got a pond at home just full of them. They drive me crazy night and day." After they made an agreement for several hundred frog legs, the farmer came back a week later with two scrawny sets of frog legs and a foolish look on his face. "I guess I was wrong," he stammered. "There were just two frogs in the pond, but they sure were making a lot of noise!"

That night I learned something. Not only did I find out that we had one very vocal person, but I also discovered that problem carriers spread their poison far and wide. And guess what? The next several times a negative comment came up at a meeting, we discovered it was the same complainer again. If you're a leader and someone tells you there are "lots of complaints," then find out the source. It may turn out to be one person doing lots of complaining.

What is your attitude and reaction toward people who voice complaints? Why?

_____

_____

_____

2. Bob Is a Problem Finder

Bob also likes to find problems and expose them to others. He subscribes to Chisholm's Second Law, which says, "Any time things appear to be going better, you have overlooked something."

Because some people have this tendency, I developed a rule for staff members. Anyone who brings me a problem must also bring three possible solutions to solve it. It doesn't take great talent to see a problem. In fact, if you look hard enough, people can find a problem in every solution. It takes greater talent to solve problems. Most Bobs have no interest in doing that.

How would presenting solutions along with the problem affect your team?

_____

_____

_____

3. Bob Is a Problem Creator

Bob always creates problems, and he usually involves others in what he's doing. He's like the guy in the corny joke who brags to some friends, "Yes, there is a proud fighting tradition in my family! My great-great-grandfather stood his ground at Bunker Hill. My great-grandfather valiantly joined up with the troops to destroy the Germans. My grandfather was at Pearl Harbor. And my father fought the North Koreans. 'Mercy!' one of his friends remarked. 'Can't your family get along with anyone?'"

What does a "problem creator" look like?

_____

_____

_____

4. Bob Is a Problem Receiver

Bob is usually a recipient of problems from others, and he encourages people to bring him more. And of course, sometimes the person is a Bobbie instead of a Bob. I had one in an organization I led years ago; I'll call her "Betty." After putting out a bunch of fires, I found that every issue somehow or another was connected to Betty. I called her into my office to have a talk. I recounted what I had found, she admitted her part in it, and we talked about it.

"People just bring me their problems all the time," she said. "I don't ask for them; they just do it."

"Do you want to know why?" I asked.

"Why, yes," Betty answered, "I would."

"People see you as a garbage dump," I answered. "Garbage trucks take their loads of trash to a place that accepts garbage. And people with problems take their gripes, gossip, and grumbling to someone who'll accept it. Because you allow people to dump on you and make no effort to stop them, they keep dumping. And they won't stop until you let them know they're not welcome." I'm sorry to say that Betty didn't change. She continued to let people back up to her desk and dump their emotional garbage in her lap.

Have you unwittingly allowed people to dump their problems on you? If so, how can you go about getting them to stop?

_____

_____

_____

WHAT ABOUT BOB?

So what do you do if you have a Bob or Bobbie in your life, someone who finds, creates, and spreads problems? Consider these suggestions:

Respond with a Positive Comment

When a negative person tries to drop a problem in your lap, respond with something positive. If the comment is about a situation, try to find the bright side. If it's about a person, point out a positive trait you've observed.

Show Your Concern for Someone Being Criticized

Anytime a person's motives are being critiqued, the best thing is to give him the benefit of the doubt. No one should presume to know the heart of another person. That's something only God can judge. Believe the best in others (and express that belief) unless the individuals prove otherwise to you personally.

Encourage Steps Toward Resolution

Anytime someone brings you a problem he has with another person—and he hasn't personally addressed the problem with the other person—he's really engaging in gossip. And if you listen, you are, too.

The best way to deal with gossip is to direct the complainer to talk to the person with whom he has an issue. Encourage them to meet one-on-one and work things out. And if he brings up the issue again, ask him point-blank: "Have you addressed this with him yet?" If the answer is no, refuse to discuss it.

Ask Bob to THINK Before Speaking

Not everyone will respond positively to your suggestions. But if you have a strong connection with Bob or you are in a position of authority with him, then ask him to THINK before he speaks using this acronym:

T—Is it true?
H—Is it helpful?
I—Is it inspiring?
N—Is it necessary?
K—Is it kind?

If he can answer yes to all of these questions, then it's appropriate for him to proceed.

Keep Bob Away from Others

Former major-league baseball manager Casey Stengel had some great advice concerning how to deal with problem people. He said that on most teams, a manager will have fifteen players who will run through a wall for him, five who hate him, and five who are undecided. He believed the trick was to keep the five who hate him away from the five who are undecided.

If you supervise one or more Bobs—and you can't or won't remove them from your team—then do damage control by isolating them. Don't let their negativism spread.

APPLYING THE BOB PRINCIPLE

1. Why is gossip so appealing to many people? How can you tell when something you are being told is gossip? What can you do to kindly stop someone from gossiping to you?

   _____

   _____

   _____

2. Think about the last time you were confronted by a people-related problem. How did you respond to it? Did the problem end there, or did it continue to smolder? Would you say that your response put water or gasoline on the "fire"? Why? How could you have responded better?

_____

_____

_____

3. Is every person who brings you a problem without offering solutions automatically a Bob or Bobbie? How often is this problem an attitude? How often is it training-related? When you've adequately trained people to seek solutions and an individual still insists on pointing out problems without offering solutions, what should you do? What will happen if you ignore the behavior?

_____

_____

_____

4. In the past, how have you handled it when a friend or colleague has come to you saying that someone else has a problem with something you have done? Was the outcome positive or negative? What happened to the relationships? How would you handle it in the future?

_____

_____

_____

5. Do you find it difficult or easy to give people the benefit of the doubt, assuming their motives to be good? Why? Which is worse: accusing a good person of bad motives, or assuming a bad person has good motives? How does your attitude in this area affect your relationships? How will you conduct yourself in the future, and why?

_____

_____

_____

Summary

I've said a lot about what to do if you have a Bob in your life, but what if _you_ are Bob? If you're not sure, ask yourself these questions:

- *Do I experience some kind of conflict almost every day?*
- *Do people often rub me the wrong way?*
- *Do bad things just naturally happen to me?*
- *Do I have few friends and wish I had more?*
- *Do I always seem to say the wrong thing?*

If you answered yes to several of these questions, then you might be Bob (or Bobbie). If that's true, remember the first rule of holes. When you're in one, stop digging.

The first thing you have to do is to admit you're Bob. The second is that you must *want* to change your lifestyle. And changing won't necessarily be easy. Begin by following the guidelines I've already given. Use the THINK questions before you speak. Try to see the positive in every situation. And ask people to hold you accountable for your attitude and actions. No one has to be a Bob forever.

THE APPROACHABILITY
PRINCIPLE

Being at Ease
with Ourselves Helps Others
Be at Ease with Us

We can give no greater gift to others than putting them at ease.

THE QUESTION I MUST ASK MYSELF:
WOULD MY FRIENDS SAY THAT I AM EASY
TO APPROACH ABOUT DIFFICULT ISSUES?

Have you ever met anyone famous? What was it like? Was it exciting, or did it turn out to be surprisingly ordinary? Were you disappointed, or was it even better than you expected? Did you connect with the person, or were you treated like a nuisance? Or were you so intimidated that you were unable to even try to talk to the person? The quality of any first-time meeting experience—whether or not people are famous—depends largely on their approachability.

We've all met people who seemed cold and forbidding. And we've all met people who treat us like old friends from day one. This isn't an issue with just high-profile people. How approachable are the most important people in your life? When you need to ask your boss a question, is it easy or difficult? When you need to talk to your spouse about a difficult subject, do you expect a dialogue or a fight? Can you bring up a touchy issue with your closest friend without worrying about being blown out of the water?

For that matter, what about you? Can the people closest to you talk to you about nearly anything? When was the last time someone brought you bad news? Or strongly disagreed with your point of view on an issue? Or confronted you concerning something you did wrong? If it has been a while, you may not be a very approachable person.

Some people treat the idea of becoming approachable as frivolous; it's a nice thing if one can be bothered to cultivate it. But truly it's much more than that. It is a powerful asset to have in one's relational toolbox. Here's the story of someone who's made that quality a $12 million-a-year asset!

WHO COULDN'T TALK TO HER?

Oprah Winfrey calls this person her idol and mentor. She is the highest-paid news personality on television, making more than Peter Jennings, Dan Rather, Tom Brokaw, Katie Couric, or anyone else. She has received numerous Emmys, a Peabody Award, the Overseas Press Club's President's Award, the International Radio and Television Society's Broadcaster of the Year Award, the Academy of Television Arts and Sciences Lifetime Achievement Award, numerous honorary degrees, and induction into the Academy of Television Arts and Sciences Hall of Fame. Her specials have run for more than twenty consecutive years. And one of her interviews became the highest-rated news program ever broadcast by a single network.[1] She is Barbara Walters. And why does she get paid the big bucks? Because *anybody* can talk to her about nearly *anything*. She is the most approachable newsperson in America.

OBSCURE BEGINNING

When Walters started out in her career, few people would have guessed her future. Walters herself said, "I was the kind nobody thought could make it. I had a funny Boston accent. I couldn't pronounce my Rs. I wasn't a beauty."[2] After graduating from Sarah Lawrence College with a degree in English, she went to work to help her financially ailing family. She worked first as a secretary and then as a writer on *Jack Parr* and *The Dick Van Dyke Show*. Then in 1961, she got a chance to write and do research for the *Today Show*. Three years later, she started working in front of the cameras as the "Today girl."

During the next thirteen years, Walters built her credibility as a journalist. She was one of a handful of journalists invited to make the historic trip to China with President Nixon in 1972. And in 1976 she became the first female co-anchor of a network evening news program. But her greatest recognition came as an interviewer. In fact, Walters has written a book called *How to Talk with Practically Anybody About Practically Anything*.

Walters has interviewed more statesmen and stars than any other television journalist in history. She has interviewed every president since Nixon. She won the first joint interview of Egypt's President Anwar Sadat and Israel's Prime Minister Menachem Begin. She has interviewed foreign leaders such as Jiang Zemin, Boris Yeltsin, Margaret Thatcher and figures such as Yasser Arafat, Saddam Hussein, Muammar Qaddafi, and Fidel Castro. And she's talked with just about any movie or television star she's wanted to.

Bill Geddie, the producer of her television specials, observes, "She has a way that has matured over the years of getting people to say things on the air that they never thought they were going to say."[3] Walters says that her favorite interviews are with people facing great adversity, such as Steven McDonald, a paralyzed police officer; Dave Dravecky, a baseball pitcher diagnosed with cancer; and the late Christopher Reeve, an actor who was a quadriplegic. It's said that her skill as an interviewer comes from the empathy and compassion she developed caring for her disabled sister, Jacqueline. Those qualities undoubtedly help, but what it really boils down to is trust. People trust Walters, so they talk to her.

DON'T MISS OUT

People miss many opportunities for connection and the chance to build deeper relationships because they do not make themselves approachable. And notice that I am purposely using the phrase "make themselves." Approachability has little to do with other people's boldness or timidity. It has everything to do with how you conduct yourself and what messages you send to others.

Years ago I saw a piece called "The Art of Getting Along," which stated,

Sooner or later, a man, if he is wise, discovers that life is a mixture of good days and bad, victory and defeat, give and take. He learns that it doesn't pay to be a too-sensitive soul, that he should let some things go over his head like water off a duck's back. He learns that he who loses his temper usually loses out, that all men have burnt toast for breakfast now and then, and that he shouldn't take the other fellow's grouch too seriously.

He learns that carrying a chip on his shoulder is the easiest way to get into trouble, that the quickest way to become unpopular is to carry tales of gossip about others, that buck-passing always turns out to be a boomerang, that it doesn't matter so much who gets the credit so long as the job gets done.

He learns that most others are as ambitious as he is, that they have brains as good or better, that hard work, not cleverness, is the secret of success. He learns that no man ever gets to first base alone, and that it is only through cooperative effort that we move on to better things.

He realizes (in short) that the "art of getting along" depends about 98 percent on his own behavior toward others.[4]

If you want to make yourself agreeable and approachable to others, then you need to put them at ease. Here's how.

HOW TO PUT PEOPLE AT EASE

Think about all the approachable people you've ever met, and I believe you'll find that they usually exhibit the following seven characteristics:

1. Personal Warmth—They Truly Like People

You can always tell when someone doesn't like people. Conversely you can feel it when individuals genuinely care for people. They are warm and kind. And as Christian

Bovee said, "Kindness is a language the dumb can speak and the deaf can hear and understand."

There's an old *Peanuts* comic strip in which Charlie Brown says, "I love mankind, it's just people I can't stand." To be approachable, it's not enough to love people in theory. You need to generate personal warmth toward the people you meet.

How do you express personal warmth toward people?

_____

_____

_____

2. Appreciation for the Differences in People

I have to admit, there was a time in my life when I had little patience for people who were very different from me. I tended to look down on people who didn't have my strengths. Then I read *Personality Plus* by Florence Littauer.[5] That book really opened my eyes. My wife, Margaret, and I read it at the same time, and we laughed as we read about each other's weaknesses and celebrated each other's strengths. As we read about each personality type defined in the book—melancholic, choleric, sanguine, and phlegmatic—we recognized friends, family members, and ourselves.

I looked at people differently after that, and I finally understood that different was good. I came to appreciate people for who they were and what they had to offer. I had a better handle on my weaknesses and how people can complement and help each other. Not only has it made me like people more, but it has also made me more likable. Appreciating the differences of others can do the same for you.

How do you tend to react to people with different personalities than your own?

_____

_____

_____

3. Consistency of Mood

Have you ever worked with or for someone whose moods were up and down all the time, and people tiptoed into the office every morning and whispered to a coworker, "How is he/she today?" With those kinds of people, you never know what you're going to get. And as a result, those kinds of people are never approachable.

In contrast, approachable people display a consistency of mood. They are even-keeled and predictable. You know what you're going to get because they are basically the same every time you see them.

Would the people you work with consider your mood consistent? Explain.

_____

_____

_____

4. Sensitivity Toward People's Feelings

Although approachable people are emotionally steady, that doesn't mean they expect others to be that way. They recognize that other people's moods are going to be different from their own. Consequently they tune in to the moods and feelings of others, and they quickly make adjustments to how they relate to others. They are like the captain of a sailboat who tests the wind and adjusts the sails according to current conditions in order to get where he desires to go.

Irish novelist George Moore recognized that "our ideas are here today and gone tomorrow, whereas our feelings are always with us, and we recognize those who feel like us, and at once, by a sort of instinct." When people sense that another person is on their wavelength, they are more likely to open up to him because he seems approachable.

How do you adapt to the moods of the people around you?

_____

_____

_____

5. Understanding of Human Weaknesses and Exposure of Their Own

Nothing is quite as off-putting as someone trying to keep up the pretense of being perfect and humorlessly trying to convince you that he's telling the truth. I remember one time in a conference I was teaching, I exhorted the leaders in attendance to admit their weaknesses to those working with them. During the break, a man approached me to say that he didn't think my suggestion was a good idea.

"Won't that make my people unsure of me?" he asked.

"No, it won't," I answered. "You see, you're operating under the assumption that they don't already know."

Ed Howe wisely advised, "Express a mean opinion of yourself occasionally; it will show your friends that you know how to tell the truth." Approachable people are honest about their abilities—and shortcomings. They are willing to be told not what they want to hear but what they need to hear. And they are able to laugh at themselves. They embrace this old Chinese proverb: "Blessed are they who can laugh at themselves. They shall never cease to be amused." And because they can admit their faults, they don't have a problem allowing other people to have faults of their own.

Write down some of your faults. How could admitting your faults or mistakes help you to build relationships with the people on your team?

_____

_____

_____

6. Ability to Forgive Easily and Ask Quickly for Forgiveness

An understanding of human weaknesses and a willingness to reveal their own make approachable people humble. And because they're humble, they quickly ask forgiveness and easily grant it to others.

Author and teacher David Augsburger wrote, "Since nothing we intend is ever fault-less, and nothing we attempt ever without error, and nothing we achieve without some measure of finitude and fallibility we call humanness, we are saved by forgiveness."[6]

Are you quick to forgive? Why or why not?

_____

_____

_____

7. Authenticity

One thing that Barbara Walters used to recite to herself anytime she was feeling uncomfortable or insecure is a statement told to her by Mrs. Eugene McCarthy: "I am the way I am; I look the way I look; I am my age."[7]

Approachable people are real. They are who they are. As a result, they engage with others on a genuine level. They don't pretend to be someone they're not. They don't go out of their way to hide what they think and feel. And they have no hidden agenda.

They say what they mean and mean what they say. You don't have to worry about where you stand with them.

Do you put up a front with others, or is what they see what they get? Explain.

_____

_____

_____

One of the reasons they can be authentic is that they are secure with themselves. Secure people don't feel that they always have to win, and they don't have anything to prove. Security is the most disarming of all traits. Approachable people are at ease with themselves, and that puts others at ease.

APPLYING THE APPROACHABILITY PRINCIPLE

1. How at ease are you with yourself? Are you basically secure or insecure? Are you confident in your abilities, or do you deal with a lot of self-doubt? Do you feel good about yourself, or do you wish you were more like someone else? Explain.

_____

_____

_____

2. Do you agree or disagree that the person who is in authority has the responsibility for putting others at ease? Explain. What happens when the weaker person must try to connect with an authoritative person who is uninterested in connection?

_____

_____

_____

3. How can you tell when someone has a hidden agenda? What kinds of things happen when that agenda is revealed? Does the possibility of having to deal with a hidden agenda make you reluctant to be open and approachable?

_____

_____

_____

4. Think about a moody person you've had to deal with in the past. What kind of an impact did that person's moods have on you? How did it affect the relationship? When are you prone to moodiness? What can you do to make your moods fluctuate less?

_____

_____

_____

5. Many people who are not approachable have no idea that others find them intimidating or standoffish. Do a 360-degree survey of your approachability. Find out if your bosses, employees, colleagues, and family members find you easy to talk to. Ask them to tell you the last time they heard you give an honest assessment of yourself. Ask them to share one of your weaknesses with you and see how you react. Your response will reveal a lot.

_____

_____

_____

Summary

Approachability is the responsibility of the one in authority! Barbara Walters is the one in authority when she does interviews, so she takes it upon herself to be approachable. Bosses must take responsibility for being approachable to their employees. Parents must make themselves approachable to their children. And spouses must be approachable to each other. Strive to be authentic, forgiving, and warm toward those around you. These characteristics will make your current relationships easier and open the door to new relationships in the future.

THE FOXHOLE PRINCIPLE

WHEN PREPARING FOR BATTLE, DIG A HOLE BIG ENOUGH FOR A FRIEND

*In poverty and other misfortunes of life, true friends are a sure refuge.
The young they keep out of mischief; to the old they are a comfort and aid
in their weakness, and those in the prime of life they incite to noble deeds.*

—ARISTOTLE

THE QUESTION I MUST ASK MYSELF:
AM I A FRIEND THAT OTHERS DEPEND
ON DURING DIFFICULT TIMES?

A few years ago, I heard pastor and Dallas Theological Seminary Chancellor Chuck Swindoll say that in the U.S. Marines he was taught to dig a foxhole big enough for a friend. That comment stuck with me because I thought it was a great insight.

If you look at an infantry training manual, you'll find that there are several kinds of foxholes (or "fighting holes" as the Marines now call them). A soldier may find himself taking up a "hasty fighting position," where he is simply scrambling for cover with no time to prepare. Or if he has time, he can dig in a position for only himself. However, experts advise that a "one-soldier fighting position . . . does not have the security of a two-soldier position." Even better is said to be an arrangement where three people can fight together. The *Army Field Manual* points out its efficiency: "One soldier can provide security; one can do priority work; and one can rest, eat, or perform maintenance. This allows the priority of work to be completed more quickly than in a one-soldier or two-soldier position." It also adds succinctly, "It is more difficult for the enemy to destroy this type position. To do so, the enemy must kill or suppress three soldiers."[1]

The power of people sticking together has been extolled for thousands of years. Solomon of ancient Israel wrote,

> Two are better than one,
> Because they have a good reward for their labor.
> For if they fall, one will lift up his companion.
> But woe to him who is alone when he falls,
> For he has no one to help him up.
> Again, if two lie down together, they will keep warm;
> But how can one be warm alone?
> Though one may be overpowered by another, two can withstand him.
> And a threefold cord is not quickly broken.[2]

Unlike Chuck Swindoll, I never served in the military. But one doesn't have to be a soldier to appreciate the benefit of having good friends during tough times. That is of value not only in the Army, but also at home or work. It's indispensable even in the high-tech world of the Internet. A good example can be seen in the history of the company Yahoo!

At First Just Two Men in the "Foxhole"

Yahoo! started out in February 1994 as the hobby of two Stanford graduate students: Jerry Yang and David Filo. The two electrical engineering students created a directory to keep track of their favorite Internet Web sites. Before long they began sharing it with others. At first it was called "Jerry's Guide to the World Wide Web." But when Yang thought that "David was doing all the work and I was getting all the credit," he changed the name to "David and Jerry's Guide to the World Wide Web."[3] Later recognizing that they needed something less cumbersome, they called it simply Yahoo!.

At first they offered two basic services: a directory of Web sites (similar to a book's table of contents) and an Internet search engine (similar to an index). Using Yahoo!, people were finally better able to find specific information on the Internet. By the fall of 1994, more than 100,000 people were using their service.

Yang and Filo knew an opportunity when they saw one. They incorporated Yahoo! in March 1995 and quickly secured $2 million from Sequoia Capital to bankroll their organization. The friends were ready to engage in a marketplace battle. They were already practicing the Foxhole Principle, having decided to work together. But they also knew they couldn't succeed on their own. So they shopped for a management team. The person they brought into the organization with them to become CEO was Tim Koogle (known as T. K.). Koogle brought in Jeffrey Mallett as COO. The four men worked together closely, but the ones who really made things happen were Koogle, Mallett, and Yang. People called them the three musketeers.

"I'm usually the pragmatic one," said Mallett, "Jerry is the untethered one and T. K. makes the final call. I just know we are always thinking about and anticipating our next moves."[4] And when Yahoo! had to face "Eisner, Welch, and Gates . . . moving directly into our space," as Mallett described it, they stuck together and fought it out. While many other dot-com companies folded, Yahoo! kept going strong.

Koogle and Mallett have since moved on to other ventures, but they have done so with no hard feelings and no regrets. Together with Yang and Filo, they helped to transform Yahoo! from a business with fewer than ten employees to a publicly traded multimillion-dollar enterprise. Today Yahoo! serves the largest worldwide audience—

well over 200 million users each month—and serves as a global branded network to its customers.[5]

The Facts about Foxholes

We face many kinds of battles in life, and the "foxholes" we sometimes inhabit come in many shapes and sizes. The home is the most important one. (Ideally it should always be a safe haven with people we can depend on.) But others may include a business, a sports team, a small group, a platoon, or something else. And of course, the people who accompany us in these places are as varied as they are.

What battles do you face? In what areas have you already dug "foxholes"?

_____

_____

_____

Before going any farther, I need to share with you three assumptions I'm making as I write about the Foxhole Principle:

1. *The foxhole is for you and a friend—not a friend alone.* You can ask a friend to fight with you, but you should never send someone else to fight your battles. When Jerry Yang and David Filo hired Tim Koogle, they didn't walk away from their responsibilities at Yahoo! They partnered with him.

2. *Before the battle, you have developed a friendship.* The Foxhole Principle is not about imposing on distant acquaintances or using people. You need to be a friend before you ask for the help of a friend.

3. *You have also been in your friends' foxholes with them.* You should be willing to fight for any friend whose help you would request. That's what friends do. Civil rights leader Martin Luther King, Jr. said, "In the end, we will remember not the words of our enemies, but the silence of our friends." I don't ever want it to be said that I was a silent friend!

Having established that, here are some truths about "foxholes":

Foxholes Without Friends Are Unhealthy

Separating oneself from others and trying to face the world alone are not healthy or help-ful. Several years ago, I read about a campaign initiated by the California Department of Mental Health with the slogan "Friends can be good medicine." Here are just a few find-ings that prompted the department to embark on the initiative:

- If you isolate yourself from others, you are two to three times more likely to die an early death. This is true independently of whether you take good care of yourself by exercising and refraining from smoking.
- If you isolate yourself from others, you are more likely to contract terminal cancer.
- If you are divorced, separated, or widowed, you have a five to ten times greater chance of being hospitalized for a mental disorder than if you are married.
- If you are a pregnant woman without good personal relationships, your chances of having some kind of complication are three times as great as those with strong relationships, even given the same amount of stress.[6]

Why is it that friends can be good medicine? Has that been true for you?

_____

_____

_____

Foxhole Experiences Forge Great Friendships

Back in the 1980s when I was looking for someone to help me figure out how to navi-gate the difficult job of pastoring a large church while leading a national ministry at the same time, Jack Hayford entered my life. Jack, who pastors the Church on the Way in Van Nuys, California, was a good friend, a wise counselor, and an unselfish mentor. I could not have succeeded without his help.

More than a decade later, I fought a much more serious battle: I suffered a major heart attack. When Jack heard about it, he called me. He told me that I was working too hard and that I would have to learn to say no to people. And then Jack said something I'll never forget. "John, I know you find it difficult to say no to some people. Have them call me; I'll say no for you. And I'll keep you out of those situations." Jack has truly been a foxhole friend to me. And recently when Jack's son-in-law died unexpectedly, I crawled into his foxhole with him. It was the least I could do after all he'd done for me.

Describe a situation where a friendship has grown because you and your friend faced a challenge together.

_____

_____

_____

Foxholes Prove Friendships

When you face tough times, you find out who your real friends are. When Pepper Rodgers was coaching at UCLA, he had some difficult seasons. Recalling an especially bad year, Rodgers told a reporter, "My dog was about my only friend, and I told my wife that man needs at least two friends. She bought me another dog."

False friends are like our shadows, keeping close to us while we walk in the sunshine but leaving us when we cross into the shade. Real friends stick with us when trouble comes. As the old saying goes: in prosperity our friends know us; in adversity we know our friends.

How does it make you feel when your friends don't stick with you in troubling times? Do you still consider them your friends? Why or why not?

_____

_____

_____

A FRIEND INDEED

It's said that when Benjamin Franklin signed the Declaration of Independence, he uttered the words, "We must, indeed, all hang together or, most assuredly, we shall hang separately." He understood the power of maintaining strong alliances during times of great conflict. By all accounts, Franklin was a faithful friend and dependable ally to his fellow countrymen throughout his life.

You may have many friends, but not all of them will be foxhole friends. For that matter, you will not be that kind of an ally to everyone in your life either. Foxhole friendships are special. Here are five things you should keep in mind before you agree to do battle with someone:

1. Foxhole Friends Are Few

During the Civil War, President Lincoln received many requests for pardons from soldiers who were sentenced to die for desertion. Each appeal was frequently accompanied by numerous testimonial letters from friends and powerful people.

One day the president received an appeal for a pardon that stood out; it arrived without a single document or letter vouching for the prisoner. Lincoln was surprised by this and asked the officer in charge about it. To Lincoln's amazement, the officer on duty said that the soldier had not one friend and that his entire family had been killed in the war. The president considered that piece of information and told the officer that he would render a decision on the matter in the morning.

Lincoln wrestled with the issue all night. Desertion was no small matter. Overruling a death sentence would send the wrong message to other soldiers. Yet he found it difficult not to have sympathy for someone so alone in the world.

In the morning when the officer asked the president for his decision, he was shocked to hear Lincoln say that the testimony of a friend had sealed his decision on the soldier in question. When the officer reminded the president that the request had come with no letter of reference, Lincoln simply stated, "I will be his friend." He then signed the request and pardoned the man.

If there are people in your life who would go to battle with you, value them, for they are rare indeed.

Who would go to battle with you? How do you nurture these friendships?

_____

_____

_____

2. Foxhole Friends Provide Strength Before and During the Battle

Having someone beside you fighting during a battle is a great help. But even before the battle, simply knowing that someone believes in you and will fight for you is uplifting. Greek philosopher Epicurus stated, "It is not so much our friends' help that helps us, as the confident knowledge that they will help us."

Think about a parent, teacher, boss, or coach who went out of the way to express belief in you. Wasn't it great to be trusted? Didn't such a person have a great impact on your life? If so, take the time to thank that individual. And make the same kind of investment of trust in the people for whom you would fight.

3. Foxhole Friends See Things from the Same Perspective

Five-year-old Tracy asked her dad if she could play at a friend's house. Her father told her she could as long as she was home by six o'clock for dinner.

When six o'clock rolled around, Tracy was nowhere to be seen. So her father waited. After about twenty-five minutes, Tracy opened the front door. Her father, working to control his impatience, asked her where she'd been.

"I'm sorry I'm late, Dad," she responded, "but my friend's doll broke right when I was supposed to leave for home."

"Oh, I see," her dad said. "And I suppose you were helping her fix it?"

"No," replied Tracy. "I was helping her cry."

People who climb down into the foxhole with you see things from your point of view, and they express empathy for your situation. That makes them not only a great help, but also a great comfort.

What do you do in order to see things from your friends' point of view when they are facing troubles?

_____

_____

_____

4. Foxhole Friends Make a Difference in Our Lives

The people who fight the great battles of life with us make a huge impact on our lives. I mentioned that I had a heart attack on December 18, 1998. In the early morning hours while I was battling for my life, a phone call from my assistant, Linda Eggers, prompted a man I barely knew to climb into the foxhole with me and save my life. Months before, I'd had lunch with Dr. John Bright Cage, a Nashville cardiologist who offered to help me "in any way he could" because he was concerned about my health. Linda called him, he called a colleague in Atlanta named Dr. Jeff Marshall, and Dr. Marshall saved my life. It was a case where a relationship literally meant the difference between life and death.

How has a foxhole friend made a difference in your life?

_____

_____

_____

5. Foxhole Friends Love Us Unconditionally

It's said that a friend is someone . . .

- who will keep your secrets and never divulge them—even if tortured or tempted with chocolate (or in my wife's case, Krispy Kreme Doughnuts©).
- who will quietly destroy the photograph that makes you look like a beached whale.
- who knows you don't know what you're talking about but will let you reach that conclusion independently.
- who goes on the same diet with you—and off it with you, too.

Foxhole friends are that—and then some. They'd face any danger with you. They'd do anything for you. They'd give anything of theirs to you.

APPLYING THE FOXHOLE PRINCIPLE

1. What makes a person willing to fight another person's battle with him? Is it always because of unselfish motives? Do motives matter? Do they change the end result?

_____

_____

_____

2. Where does empathy come into play in the Foxhole Principle? Does it develop before the people get together or after they've begun to fight? What other factors, such as values, priorities, vision, etc., might come into play?

_____

_____

_____

3. What kind of a friend have you been to others? Have you been "in the foxhole" with a friend, colleague, or family member? How do you decide whether to become that kind of a friend to somebody?

_____

_____

_____

4. Why do you think some people "climb into the foxhole" alone? Is it something they do because they prefer it or because they have not sufficiently built relationships? What happens to a person who must continually fight alone?

_____

_____

_____

5. In what kinds of situations are you more likely to develop a friendship before doing battle together? In what situations are you likely to find yourself doing battle as a matter of survival and developing a friendship along the way? Do both situations lead to equally deep or long-lasting relationships? Explain.

_____

_____

_____

Summary

Author and former pastor of City Temple in London, Leslie D. Weatherhead, wrote about two friends who were literally foxhole friends; they were soldiers together. He said that when one of the soldiers was injured and could not get back to safety, his buddy went out to get him, against his officer's orders. He returned mortally wounded, and his friend, whom he had carried back, was dead.

The officer was angry. "I told you not to go," he said. "Now I've lost both of you. It was not worth it."

The dying man replied, "But it was, sir, because when I got to him, he said, 'Jim, I knew you'd come.'"

Unlike what these two men faced, the conflicts you face may not be on the battle-field. They may not be life and death. But no matter what, wouldn't you prefer to face them with a friend at your side? If so, be a foxhole friend to others, the kind of friend that others can trust, no matter what.

THE INVESTMENT QUESTION
ARE WE WILLING TO INVEST
IN OTHERS?

No man can live happily who regards himself alone; who turns everything to his own advantage. You must live for others if you wish to live for yourself.

—SENECA

Individuals who learn the People Principles that prepare them to answer the questions in the first three sections of this book—

Readiness: Are we prepared for relationships?
Connection: Are we willing to focus on others?
Trust: Can we build mutual trust?

—can consider themselves to be in pretty good shape relationally. They will have become prepared emotionally for relationships by letting go of their personal baggage. They will be able to connect well with others. And they will be capable of engendering trust when dealing with others. Most people who interact with them will consider them to possess excellent people skills. However, if they stop there, they will miss the best part of relationships.

That brings us to the investment question: Are we willing to invest in others? You may be wondering why I think that is so important. You may even be asking, "Why would anyone take the time and energy to invest in others?" To discover the answer, think about this:

You may build a beautiful house, but eventually it will crumble.
You may develop a fine career, but one day it will be over.
You may save a great sum of money, but you can't take it with you.
You may be in superb health today, but in time it will decline.
You may take pride in your accomplishments, but someone will surpass you.

So many people invest in these things, but they are transitory. So what can you possibly invest in that will last? People! When it comes right down to it, is there anything else that really matters in this world compared to people?

Relationships are like anything else. The return you get depends on what you invest. Sometimes when I speak at conferences, young leaders come up to me and say, "I would love to do what you do. How do I get a gig like this?"

Honestly that question makes me chuckle. Sometimes I respond, "You may want to do what I do, but would you like to do what I did in order to do what I do?" They see the bright lights and the big auditorium. But they don't see the decades I spent teaching small groups of people for the mere love of it because it didn't pay anything. They don't see the hundreds of times that my wife, Margaret, and I hauled grungy boxes filled with books and notebooks on and off airplanes before we could afford to hire any help. They don't consider the thousands of hours we've spent traveling, and the uncomfortable hotel rooms and bad meals. The real work has always been behind the scenes. What they see today is really the culmination of thirty years of hard work outside the spotlight.

That's the way the best relationships are. They take work behind the scenes. Once you've gotten to know people, learn to invest in them. The best relationships are always the result of unselfish giving. The following five People Principles offer insight on some of the most important ways we can invest in relationships:

The Gardening Principle: All relationships need cultivation.

The 101 Percent Principle: Find the 1 percent we agree on and give it 100 percent of our effort.

The Patience Principle: The journey with others is slower than the journey alone.

The Celebration Principle: The true test of relationships is not only how loyal we are when friends fail, but also how thrilled we are when they succeed.

The High Road Principle: We go to a higher level when we treat others better than they treat us.

If you can answer the investment question in a positive way, then your relationships will begin going to a whole new level.

THE GARDENING PRINCIPLE

ALL RELATIONSHIPS
NEED CULTIVATION

Friendship is like money, easier made than kept.

—SAMUEL BUTLER

THE QUESTION I MUST ASK MYSELF:
DO I OCCASIONALLY OR CONTINUALLY
CULTIVATE MY RELATIONSHIPS?

In 1997, sportswriter Mitch Albom wrote a book called *Tuesdays with Morrie*. It contains the wisdom of recollections of Morrie Schwartz, Albom's former college professor and mentor who was dying of Lou Gehrig's disease. After seeing an interview Schwartz did with Ted Koppel on *Nightline* in 1995, Albom reconnected with Schwartz after a twenty-year hiatus and cultivated a deeper relationship with him. *Tuesdays with Morrie* came as a result of their meetings. It was a runaway bestseller that stayed on the *New York Times* bestseller list for four years. As of March 2004, it had more than 5 million copies in print, was published in thirty languages in thirty-four countries, and had been made into an Emmy-winning movie.[1]

THE NEXT STORY

Albom's readers were eager to see how he would follow up his bestseller. Most people wanted him to write a sequel. "After *Tuesdays with Morrie*," says Albom, "I was inundated with offers to do *Wednesdays with Morrie, Thursdays with Morrie, Chicken Soup with Morrie*. I refused because I had said everything that I wanted to say."[2] Accordingly many people were surprised in 2003 when he published *The Five People You Meet in Heaven*, not because it wasn't about Morrie, but because unlike his previous seven books, it was a novel.

The book contains the story of eighty-three-year-old amusement park worker Eddie, who lives what he believes to be an insignificant life, but learns about his impact after he dies and reaches heaven. What's interesting is that the book was inspired by a real person: Albom's Uncle Eddie.

Albom describes Edward Beitchman as a "stumpy, thick-jawed, barrel-chested man born in 1908 to poor immigrant parents in a poor immigrant neighborhood. He was one of nine children, neither the youngest nor the oldest, only the toughest." Albom comments, "He was the champion of my family tree—and stronger than anyone I knew."[3]

Uncle Eddie was Albom's childhood hero. A World War II veteran who worked as a cab driver and factory worker, Eddie had faced down a man in his cab who wanted to kill him. Albom says that when the "nefarious rider tried to slit his throat with a knife, [Eddie] grabbed the blade and squeezed so hard, the would-be killer ran away."[4] And Eddie claimed that during emergency open-heart surgery, he had opened his eyes for a moment to see a group of dead relatives at the edge of the bed waiting for him, to which Eddie responded, "Get the hell out of here, I'm not ready for any of youse yet."[5]

Albom grew up and became a successful journalist. Although he did not keep in contact with his mentor Morrie Schwartz, he kept in contact with Uncle Eddie. He used to call the older man as he traveled around the country on assignment. And Eddie, who Albom says had lived a life of unrealized dreams, was always excited and impressed with his escapades.

Uncle Eddie made a profound impact on Albom, but Mitch never really let his uncle know about it before he died. Albom admits, "At his funeral, I delivered the eulogy. I broke down halfway through and started crying uncontrollably. It was sadness, yes, but also regret. I had never said those loving things to his face."[6]

All relationships need cultivation to grow. Mitch Albom did maintain his relationship with Eddie. But he never really took it any deeper than it had been when he was a child. And now he realizes that he missed a great opportunity.

"We all have wonderful people in our lives," notes Albom, "but when they're gone, it seems, all we can do is miss them. I miss Eddie's quiet toughness . . . I realize I have never met anyone as magical as my uncle seemed to me as a boy. He should have known that. And I wish I had told him."[7]

Whose funeral might you be asked to speak at? What would you say? Have you already shared your words of love and admiration with this person?

HOW DOES YOUR GARDEN GROW?

You cannot neglect a relationship and expect it to grow. That's not to say that all relationships are the same and need the same amount of time and attention. The nature and purpose of the relationship will determine the energy and time needed to cultivate it. Think about some of the many personal and professional relationships you have in your life. How much effort do you give them? Do you treat them the same? Of course not. And you shouldn't. Every relationship is different but can fit into one of three categories:

Some People Come into Our Lives for a Reason

Many relationships are very short and occur for very specific reasons. Sometimes they come and then go away forever. Other times they are ongoing but intermittent. These relationships need only brief, periodic cultivation.

A good example of this kind of relationship is the one with my doctor. I never would have met Dr. Jeff Marshall, my cardiologist, if it hadn't been for the heart attack I suffered in 1998. I consider him my friend as well as my doctor, but I see him only a couple of times a year. And it's always related to my health.

List a few people who came into your life for a reason, and beside their name list how they helped you.

_____

_____

_____

Some People Come into Our Lives for a Season

A second type of relationship lasts only for a period of time. These relationships may last only a few weeks or as long as several years. Many times they are related to our current circumstances or situations. But just because they are temporary doesn't mean they're not important. The cultivation of the relationships should just match the season.

Relationships with our children's teachers and coaches are often seasonal. So are many work relationships. Perhaps you work for a boss you enjoy, but the work is the only bond. And when you move on to another job, you have little reason or occasion to keep in touch. Sometimes that's just the way these relationships work out.

List the people who were in your life for a season, and explain how they helped you during that time.

_____

_____

_____

Some People Come into Our Lives for a *Lifetime*

The third kind of relationship is ongoing and permanent. These are few and very special. And if we want to keep them healthy and encourage them to grow, we must give them continual cultivation. Otherwise they are likely to shrivel and die.

Our closest friendships are most valuable to us, and like anything of value, they cost us something. We cannot neglect them and expect them to thrive. Playwright George Bernard Shaw once wrote a note to his friend Archibald Henderson that said, "I have neglected you shockingly of late. This is because I have had to neglect everything that could be neglected without immediate ruin, and partly because you have passed into the circle of intimate friends whose feelings one never dreams of considering." Shaw must have realized that his relationship with his friend was in desperate need of attention, and he desired to save it. What price can you put on a great friendship?

How often do you talk to your lifetime friends?

_____

_____

_____

The most important relationship anyone has in this world is the one with a spouse. Men and women are so different that it's not always easy to cultivate a really good relationship. I recently came across a humorous piece that pokes fun at the differences between the genders:

- A man will pay $2 for a $1 item he wants; a woman will pay $1 for a $2 item that she doesn't want.

- A woman worries about the future until she gets a husband; a man never worries about the future until he gets a wife.

- A successful man is one who makes more money than his wife can spend; a successful woman is one who can find such a man.

- To be happy with a man you must understand him a lot and love him a little; to be happy with a woman you must love her a lot and not try to understand her at all.

- Married men live longer than single men, but married men are a lot more willing to die.

- Any married man should forget his mistakes—there's no use in two people remembering the same thing.

- A woman marries a man expecting he will change, but he doesn't; a man marries a woman expecting that she won't change and she does.

- A woman has the last word in any argument; anything a man says after that is the beginning of a new argument.

- There are two times when a man doesn't understand a woman: before marriage and after.

Socrates said, "By all means marry; if you get a good wife, you'll become happy. If you get a bad one, you'll become a philosopher." Selecting the right man or woman to marry is important, but it's only part of the process of developing a good marriage. Before we marry, the focus is on a future mate. After we marry, it's on ourselves. Dating brings out the *best*—marriage brings out the *rest*.

Marriage, like any long-term relationship, requires us to . . .

- Wade through a few things that are difficult.
- Work for many things that are needed.
- Wait on some things that take time.
- Watch out for those things that can be harmful.
- Wave good-bye to personal things that are selfish.

These are all aspects of cultivation. Marriage partners who don't intentionally culti-vate a close relationship will drift apart. It's sad, but after five years of marriage, all some couples have in common is their wedding day. Some marriages may be made in heaven, but their maintenance must be done on earth.

Think about a couple you would consider to have a healthy marriage. What makes their marriage successful? How can you learn from them and build your own marriage or closest relationship?

WAYS TO KEEP CULTIVATING IMPORTANT RELATIONSHIPS

What does it mean to cultivate a relationship? Whether it's as a spouse, a parent, or a friend, you can start to cultivate a healthy, growing relationship by focusing on the following six things:

1. Commitment

Researcher Dr. Alfred Kinsey observed, "There may be nothing more important in a marriage than a determination that it shall persist. With such a determination, individuals force themselves to adjust and to accept situations which would otherwise seem sufficient grounds for a breakup." Deep commitment to the relationship is one of the greatest assets a married couple can have. But it's also a characteristic of *all* deep relationships.

Political theorist Thomas Paine asserted, "What we obtain too cheaply we esteem too little; it is dearness only that gives everything its value." Every long-lasting relationship suffers strains and setbacks. And no two people agree on everything. Even the best friendships can expect to face conflict. The question is, What are you going to do when trouble comes? How committed are you? Are you more dedicated to maintaining the relationship or to avoiding conflict? Your answer just might determine whether your relationship is lifelong or merely temporary.

What challenges have you and your spouse or closest friend worked through together? How did this affect your relationship?

_____

_____

_____

2. Communication

How can a relationship form without communication? It often *begins* with easy communication. Sometimes a spark easily ignites a friendship. It *deepens* with more difficult communication. Author Sydney J. Harris believes that "it is impossible to learn anything important about anyone until we get him or her to disagree with us; it is only in contradiction that character is disclosed." And it is *sustained* with intentional communication.

Several years after Margaret and I were married, I realized that when I got home to see her, there was no excitement in our communication. She'd ask about what had happened during the day, and I wasn't very enthusiastic about discussing it. Then I figured out why: during the course of most days, I had shared the most exciting events with a colleague or my assistant. So I was not all that excited about repeating it to Margaret. I knew that needed to change. My solution? Whenever something important or exciting happens during the day, I jot a note about it on a three-by-five card. And then I don't tell other people about it; I save it for the end of the day. That way, Margaret is the first to hear about it, and she is the recipient of my enthusiasm.

Do you agree that in disagreement a person's character is disclosed? Explain.

_____

_____

_____

3. Friendship

Critic Samuel Johnson remarked, "If a man does not make new acquaintances as he advances through life, he will soon find himself left alone; A man, sir, should keep his friendship in a constant repair." That goes for old friendships as well as new ones. I think we sometimes take for granted the people closest to us, and as a result, we neglect to try being good friends to them first.

For this reason, I remind myself constantly to be Margaret's friend first, before trying to be anything else to her. I try to put her concerns first. And when there is conflict between us or if she is in doubt about making a decision, I tell her, "I'm your best friend," to remind her that I'm looking out for her.

What actions do you take to show your spouse or best friend that he or she is important to you?

_____

_____

_____

4. Memories

I believe that shared memories are a wonderful source of connection and bonding for people. Have you ever gone to a school reunion or met up with friends you haven't seen for ten, twenty, or thirty years? What helps you to reconnect almost instantly? It's the memories of your shared experiences!

Today our children are all grown up, married, and living on their own with children of their own. But when they were in their teen years, like many parents, we were worried about their becoming disconnected from us and heading off in a direction that wasn't good for them. At the same time, we knew we needed to give them more and more freedom to be independent. One of the ways we kept the connection strong without trying to force it was by creating a family history. We traveled a lot together and did many activities designed to create positive memories. All of that gave our children something positive to reflect on when their need for independence might have driven them away.

5. Growth

Benjamin Franklin said, "Promise may get friends, but it is performance that keeps them." When you begin any friendship, it is filled with promise. But you have to find ways to keep it fresh and strong so that it continues to have potential and not just good memories. One way to do that is to grow together.

How are you and your closest friend growing together?

_____

_____

_____

6. Spoiling Each Other

Voltaire wrote, "If the first law of friendship is that it has to be cultivated, the second law is to be indulgent when the first law has been neglected." You can't go wrong spoiling anyone—except perhaps your children. And even that is hard not to do. I try to extend small kindnesses to my friends all the time. Margaret and I continually try to spoil each other. And I won't even talk about how we treat our grandchildren!

APPLYING THE GARDENING PRINCIPLE

1. Name some ways in which people in relationships can positively communicate with one another. Does the type of relationship affect which kinds of communication are appropriate? Which methods are most effective for the relationships you value most?

_____

_____

_____

2. How can a person tell the difference between a relationship that is meant to last for a season and one that has the potential to last a lifetime? How did some of your most significant long-term relationships start? With whom do you currently have a short-term relationship that has potential for something deeper? How can you test the waters to see if it can go to the next level?

_____

_____

_____

3. How do you determine with whom you spend your time? Do you think in terms of the importance of the relationship? Do you carve out time for the most significant people and then guard it carefully? Or does your calendar simply fill up on a first-come, first-served basis? Are you satisfied with what you currently do? If not, how can you improve it?

_____

_____

_____

4. The chapter mentioned the importance of wading through difficult issues. Why do people allow difficult issues to remain unresolved in important relationships? Do you think there ever are valid reasons for not dealing with them? Is there an issue between you and someone important that you have not addressed but should? When will you deal with it?

_____

_____

_____

5. When was the last time you spoiled your wife or significant other? Is that something you do often, or is it not something you think much about? Explain why. What could you do to improve in this area?

Summary

Let your friends and family members know how much you care as often as you can. Don't end up living with regrets the way Mitch Albom has concerning Uncle Eddie.

Nancy Reagan, wife of President Ronald Reagan, said, "I am a big believer that you have to nourish any relationship. I am still very much a part of my friends' lives, and they are very much a part of my life. A First Lady who does not have this source of strength and comfort can lose perspective and become isolated." That's true not only of people in the public eye; it's true for all of us. The friendships we develop with others enrich the quality of our lives. But we cannot sustain them if we don't cultivate them. That's why it's important for us to practice the Gardening Principle.

THE 101 PERCENT PRINCIPLE

FIND THE 1 PERCENT
WE AGREE ON AND GIVE IT 100
PERCENT OF OUR EFFORT

If two men on the same job agree all the time, then one is useless. If they disagree all the time, then both are useless.

—DARRYL F. ZANUCK

THE QUESTION I MUST ASK MYSELF:
CAN I FIND COMMON GROUND, AND
WILL I GIVE IT 100 PERCENT OF MY EFFORT?

Sometimes building relationships is an uphill battle, and connecting with another person can be particularly difficult. How do you connect with people when you seem to have nothing in common with them? Can you build relational bridges in such circumstances? And if so, can the relationships be healthy, long-lasting, and productive? These are legitimate questions. Let's face it. When you see no common ground with another person, it's going to be a challenge to connect. So how do you do it?

The answer can be found in the 101 Percent Principle. When connection is difficult, you must find the one thing the two of you can agree upon. You can do that with just about *anybody*. The problem is that many people naturally take the opposite approach; they look for differences. Why? Sometimes it's due to natural competitiveness; people are often looking for an edge. Sometimes it's to make themselves stand out, to find their own distinctiveness. Other times people focus on differences because they feel threatened by them.

Instead, to make a connection, people need to reach common ground. Most people have many things in common. But even the oddest couple can find something they agree on. Once they do, they need to give it 100 percent of their effort. The greater the differences, the more important it is to focus on what they agree on—and the greater the effort they need to give it. That's not always easy, but the benefits can be remarkably rewarding. This story illustrates that.

Describe a unique friendship you have developed with someone with whom you have few things in common.

_____

_____

_____

GO WEST, YOUNG MAN

Charles Howard was an entrepreneur's entrepreneur. In 1903, after serving in the United States cavalry and then working as a bicycle mechanic in New York, Howard decided to seek his fortune out West. He settled in San Francisco and managed to open a bicycle repair shop downtown.

In those days, automobiles were a new (and often unreliable) addition to the landscape. But there were no auto repair shops. For that reason, car owners began visiting Howard's shop to ask for his help. And Howard was willing to give auto repair a try. It didn't take long for Howard to see a great opportunity. He soon hopped a train to Detroit and wangled a meeting with William C. Durant, head of Buick and future founder of General Motors. Durant liked Howard and hired him. Before long, Howard held the franchise rights to sell Buicks for all of San Francisco, and in 1905 at the age of twenty-eight, Howard opened his first Buick dealership showcasing three vehicles he had purchased while in Detroit.

At first, things didn't go well for Howard, but after the earthquake and fire of 1906, he capitalized on the need for automobiles. Between his natural nose for opportunity and his mastery of promotion, he began to see great success. In 1909, Howard expanded his role in the business. He acquired sole distributorship of Buick, National, and Oldsmobile vehicles for all of the western U.S. The enterprise made the pioneer car man fabulously wealthy. And later when Durant got overextended and faced bankruptcy, Howard bailed him out with a personal loan of $190,000, which Durant later repaid with GM stock and a percentage of gross sales. Howard couldn't have been more successful. Even the crash of the stock market in 1929 didn't destroy him as it did so many others.

In the early 1930s, the old cavalryman-turned-car magnate rekindled his love of horses, and a friend got him interested in horse racing. He decided that if he was going to own thoroughbreds, he would go first class. He purchased a few horses, then looked for a trainer. The man he found was fifty-six-year-old Tom Smith, a man of the Old West. The two men could not have been more different. Where Howard was a master salesman and promoter, Smith was a quiet man who rarely spoke and could spend literally hours and days watching a horse's every movement. Where Howard was a great businessman used to every luxury, Smith was a former cowboy who was used to sleeping on the ground. Smith had been an experienced mustang hunter and horse breaker from age thirteen. During his career, he had worked as a deer hunter, sheep ranch foreman, mountain lion tracker, farrier, and horse trainer. The Native Americans called him the Lone Plainsman.

Author and racing expert Laura Hillenbrand says of Howard and Smith,

The two men stood in different halves of the century. Smith was the last of the true frontiersmen; Howard was paving Smith's West under the urgent wheels of his automobiles. Howard was driven by image; Smith remained the Lone Plainsman, forbidding and solitary.

But Howard was blessed with an uncanny eye for horsemen. He took one look at Smith and instincts rang in his head. He drove Smith to his barn and introduced his horses to their new trainer.[1]

Added to this unlikely mix was a jockey who had seen better days. John Pollard was a very tough man, even in a profession of tough men. Not only was he a rider, but he had been a prize fighter—although not a very good one. At five feet seven inches, he towered over his rival jockeys. And like many of them, he tortured his body to keep his weight below 115 pounds. In 1928, Pollard had been one of the top twenty riders in the nation. But his skills had slipped, and by the mid-1930s when Smith hired him, he was winning fewer and fewer races. At that point in his career, his distinction was that he was willing to ride horses other jockeys were afraid to touch.

How Did They Get Together?

The millionaire, the frontiersman, and the prizefighter—the three men had nothing in common, except one thing: a seemingly worthless racehorse that Smith spotted and Howard purchased. All three had the ability to focus on the one thing they had in common and not their differences.

Hillenbrand describes the horse this way:

> The colt's body, built low to the ground, had all the properties of a cinder block . . . His stubby legs were a study in unsound construction . . . Thanks to his unfortunate assembly, his walk was an odd, straddle-legged motion that was often mistaken for lameness . . . His gallop was so disorganized that he had a maddening tendency to whack himself in the front ankle with his own hind hoof . . . All of this raggedness was not helped by his racing schedule . . . Though only three years old, he had already run forty-three races, far more than most horses contest in their entire careers.[2]

The animal's name was Seabiscuit. What looked to others like an incorrigible nag became one of the most famous racehorses of all time—a national hero in the midst of the Depression when people needed to be lifted up. (In 1938, Seabiscuit was the nation's top news maker, generating more press than Franklin D. Roosevelt or Adolf Hitler!) Seabiscuit not only set a record for earnings, but in a head-to-head duel, he went on to defeat War Admiral—a Triple Crown winner and one of the best racehorses of all time.

That contest, which most experts at the time believed Seabiscuit could not win, is now considered by many to be the greatest horse race of all time.

When to Practice the 101 Percent Principle

It is truly remarkable that three such different men were able to find common ground, to find the one thing they could agree upon and invest their energy in it. But that is the value of the 101 Percent Principle. It is an incredible tool in anyone's relational toolbox. However, it's not something that can be pulled out and used all the time. I say that because this principle takes a big commitment of time, energy, and thinking. Therefore, before practicing this principle, you need to ask yourself some questions:

Is the Person Worth the Commitment?

Every person has worth, but you cannot give every person the time or energy that the 101 Percent Principle requires. So who is "worthy" of this kind of attention? The list begins with your spouse if you're married. In an area where the two of you don't agree, use the 101 Percent Principle. (Margaret and I usually don't see eye to eye on my calendar, but we do agree that we want to spend time together, so we focus on that.) Add your family members to the list. If you own a business and have partners, they must be included on the list. After that, add your friends. Beyond that circle of people, use your judgment. If there is good potential for a mutually rewarding relationship and you can afford to expend the energy, then you might want to give the 101 Percent Principle a try when you find it difficult to agree.

List your 101 Percent People.

_____

_____

_____

Is the Situation Worth the Commitment?

Most situations where disagreements occur are short-term. In such cases, keep in mind that "this too shall pass." Let it go and save your energy for scenarios where your expenditure of time and attention will have a long-term return.

Give an example of a long-term situation in which you had to find common ground in order to be successful.

_____

_____

_____

_____

Is the Issue Worth the Commitment?

When an issue touches on a priority in your life or impacts one of your values, use the 101 Percent Principle. If it doesn't, think twice. And keep in mind the words of clergyman Richard Baxter: "In necessary things, unity; in doubtful things, liberty; in all things, charity."

Is the Return Worth the Commitment?

During the first three years of Seabiscuit's life, many people had the opportunity to find his potential. In fact, before Smith trained him, Seabiscuit was in the stable of James Fitzsimmons, the most respected trainer of his day. But Fitzsimmons had so many high-caliber horses that Seabiscuit didn't seem worth the effort. Smith saw things differently, and look at the return he received!

A 101 PERCENT RETURN

Practicing the 101 Percent Principle can benefit you in many ways. Here are six:

1. It Allows You to Build a Foundation for Change

If you are in a relationship where you want to influence someone and change the way he sees or does something, then you shouldn't try to initiate the change in an area where you disagree. In relationships, change always begins with common ground. When you practice the 101 Percent Principle, you find that common ground and expand it. It becomes an excellent starting point for change.

2. It Prevents Unnecessary Conflict

I've learned that it's hard to argue with people when they're right. When you focus on the area where you agree with someone else, you are on safe ground because both are right. General Ulysses S. Grant said, "There never was a time, in my opinion, some way could not be found to prevent the drawing of a sword." Why create conflict if you can avoid it?

Do you agree with Grant that you can always "prevent the drawing of a sword"? Explain.

_____

_____

_____

3. It Reduces the Odds of Making Enemies

Ralph Waldo Emerson observed, "He who has a thousand friends has not a friend to spare, while he who has one enemy will meet him everywhere." Wouldn't you agree that even one enemy in life is more than we would care to have? The best way to get rid of a potential enemy is to make him your friend. When you look for the things you agree on, you increase the odds of doing just that.

Think of someone with whom you have trouble getting along. What do you have in common?

_____

_____

_____

4. It Keeps Something of Value that Could Have Been Lost

How many potentially rewarding relationships have you missed because you focused on differences instead of common ground? How many potential friends have slipped through your fingers? How many productive business associations have you forfeited? Former New York Yankees manager Joe McCarthy observed, "Any manager who can't get along with a .400 hitter is crazy." If you want to keep yourself open to potentially rewarding relationships, be prepared to try the 101 Percent Principle.

5. It Helps You to Feel Good about Your Part of the Relationship

Novelist Jane Austen quipped in a letter sent to her sister Cassandra, "I don't want people to be very agreeable, as it saves me the trouble of liking them." People who look for the worst in others may try to make themselves *look better* by comparison, but they rarely *feel better* about the way they handle the relationship. In contrast, people who look for the best and focus on what they agree on can take satisfaction in knowing that they did their part.

6. It Enables You to Make the Best of Difficult Situations

The happiest people don't necessarily *have* the best of everything. They just *make* the best of everything. Adopting the 101 Percent Principle makes the best of every relational opportunity. And no one can be expected to do more than that.

APPLYING THE 101 PERCENT PRINCIPLE

1. Have you ever met someone who seems to practice the 101 Percent Principle, a person who masterfully finds the common ground in relationships where people don't see eye to eye? If so, describe that person. What do you admire about him or her? What personal qualities do these people possess that make them so good at connecting with others? What percentage of people in your business or career area practices this principle?

_____

_____

_____

2. Why shouldn't you automatically embrace the 101 Percent Principle in every relationship? Which relationships in your life warrant its use? Describe how you will change your interaction with one of these people.

_____

_____

_____

3. Which situations are not worth the effort required to implement the 101 Percent Principle? Which are? Which issues are important to you? How do these issues relate to your values and priorities?

_____

_____

_____

4. Have you allowed an important relationship to slip through your fingers because you didn't find common ground upon which to connect? What are you missing as a result? How could you go about repairing the relationship? Would the return be worth the effort? What is stopping you from taking action?

_____

_____

_____

5. Think of an important relationship in your life that really needs change. Up to now, have you used a common-ground approach to building the relationship before trying to initiate change? What one thing can you and the other person agree on? How can you use that as a springboard for improving the relationship? How can you then take steps toward change that will benefit both of you?

_____

_____

_____

Summary

In the chapter on the Pain Principle, I told you the story of Rick, the man who sent me a letter criticizing my sermon every week, whom I won over after several years of effort. The way I got him to accept me was by using the 101 Percent Principle. As I mentioned, his kids and ours were adopted. The one thing I could find that we agreed on was that adopted children were special. So whenever we talked, I focused on our kids. I gave his kids special attention, praised them whenever possible, and loved them like they were my nieces and nephews. And *anytime* I was going to be around Rick, if it was appropriate, I brought my children, Elizabeth and Joel Porter, with me.

Rick's children loved me. And his wife warmed up to me quickly. Rick was still a hard nut to crack, but he couldn't hold out forever. It's hard to hold a grudge against someone your whole family likes—especially when that person has never done anything wrong to you in the first place.

Maybe you have a "Rick" in your life, someone you've never gotten along with. You easily see all the person's weaknesses and find it difficult to see anything but differences. I guarantee you that you can agree on *something*. All you have to do is to find it. And once you do, give it 100 percent of your effort. You'll be amazed by the impact it can make.

THE PATIENCE PRINCIPLE

THE JOURNEY WITH OTHERS
IS SLOWER THAN THE JOURNEY ALONE

For the friendship of two, the patience of one is necessary.

—ANONYMOUS

> THE QUESTION I MUST ASK MYSELF:
> DO I TAKE OTHERS WITH ME
> EVEN WHEN IT'S INCONVENIENT?

E very now and then, you read a story that just seems too wacky to be true. That's the case with this one about Larry Walters, a guy who took the journey alone. It's crazy, but true:

Larry's boyhood dream was to fly. But fate conspired to keep him from his dream. He joined the Air Force, but his poor eyesight disqualified him from the job of pilot. After he was discharged from the military, he sat in his backyard watching jets fly overhead.

He hatched his weather balloon scheme while sitting outside in his "extremely comfortable" Sears lawn chair. He purchased 45 weather balloons from an army-navy surplus store, tied them to his tethered lawn chair dubbed the Inspiration I, and filled the four-foot diameter balloons with helium. Then he strapped himself into his lawn chair with some sandwiches, Miller Light beer, and a pellet gun. He figured he would pop a few of the many balloons when it was time to descend.

Larry's plan was to sever the anchor and lazily float up to a height of about 30 feet above his back yard where he would enjoy a few hours of flight before coming back down. But things didn't work out as Larry planned.

When his friends cut the cord anchoring the lawn chair to his Jeep, he did not float lazily up to 30 feet. Instead, he streaked into the LA skies as if shot from a cannon, pulled by a lift of 42 helium balloons holding 33 cubic feet of helium each. He didn't level off at 100 feet, nor did he level off at 1,000 feet. After climbing and climbing, he leveled off at 16,000 feet.

At that height he felt he could not risk shooting any of the balloons, lest he unbalance the load and find himself in real trouble. So he stayed there, drifting cold and frightened with his beer and sandwiches, for more than 14 hours. He crossed the primary approach corridor of LAX, where Trans World Airlines and Delta Airlines pilots radioed in reports of the strange sight.

Eventually he gathered the nerve to shoot a few balloons, and slowly descended. The hanging tethers tangled and caught in a power line, blacking out a Long Beach neighborhood for 20 minutes. Larry climbed to safety, where he was arrested by waiting members of the

LAPD. As he was led away in handcuffs, a reporter dispatched to cover the daring rescue asked him why had he done it. Larry replied nonchalantly, "A man can't just sit around."[1]

Fortunately we don't need to go to such lengths to travel—or to get away from people.

TRAVEL TIPS

For twenty-five years I have done a lot of traveling. I've lost track of how many air miles I've logged, but it must be more than 3 million. I've been on just about every kind of aircraft (*except* a floating lawn chair), in all kinds of conditions, on six out of seven continents. And no matter where I was going or what I was doing, I've always found one thing to be true: the journey with others is always slower than the journey alone.

I was reminded of that again recently when I went on a cruise with my family. On a business trip by myself, I blaze on down to the airport, and I'm on a plane *really* quickly. I know the ins and outs of most airports, I know how to avoid lines, and I don't check bags. And if just Margaret and I are traveling together, we still move very quickly. After thirty-five years of marriage and traveling together, we have a great system. But when we go with the whole family—two children, their spouses, and all the grandchildren—believe me, it's a lot slower. And if you add my parents or Margaret's or either of our siblings or their families, it just multiplies. I love the time with family, and I wouldn't trade it, but I go into such trips *knowing* that we're going to be traveling at a slow pace.

I have to admit, patience is not one of my strengths. Every day I find myself wondering, *Why are these people moving so slowly?* It happens in traffic, in stores, at work, on the golf course, and on and on. Margaret calls me the Energizer Bunny™. The good news is that while I don't have as much energy as I did in my twenties, I still have lots of energy, even though I'm in my late fifties. The bad news is that when I was younger, I constantly cast vision for the people in my organization and then left them behind—not a good thing for a leader. I had to learn to connect with people and develop patience. These are two critical steps in relationship building:

> Patience without connection—the relationship lacks energy.
> Connection without patience—the relationship lacks potential.
> Connection with patience—the relationship has energy and potential.

If you want relationships to last, you need both energy and potential.

Would your family or close friends consider you a patient person? Why or why not?

_____

_____

_____

MAKING PATIENCE A VIRTUE

Just about everyone would agree that patience is a good quality; we admire it and desire it. Those of us who need it most are least inclined to cultivate it, however. We need patience in order to develop patience. So how do we overcome this catch-22? The answer is to develop a plan. Here are six steps you can take to become a more patient person in relationships:

1. Prioritize Patience as a Virtue Worthy of Developing

Arnold Glasgow stated, "The key to everything is patience. You get the chicken by hatching the egg, not smashing it." In the long run, you will find that patience with people is beneficial to you. But you may not see a return right away. It may be something you have to wait for. If you are an impatient person and have a hard time prioritizing patience now, then know this: the people around you will benefit from it immediately. As Greek philosopher Aristotle noted, "The greatest virtues are those which are most useful to other persons."

Give an example of a time when you benefited from being patient. Give another example when you benefited from someone being patient with you.

_____

_____

_____

2. Understand that It Takes Time to Build Good Relationships

Anything really worthwhile in this life takes time to build, and that's true of relationships. The more people involved in the relational circle, the longer it takes. For example, think about how long it takes for a work group to develop relationships and chemistry. Two or three people can get to know each other and learn to work together fairly quickly. It takes five people a lot longer. If you have nine or ten people, it really takes a lot of time for all of them to jell. The bigger the group, the longer it takes.

Relationships of any depth take time as well. Even in the best circumstances, such as when you have instant chemistry with another person, it still takes time to really build that relationship and make it strong. All good relationships take time.

How long did it take a group you are part of (at work, church, etc.) to jell? Why was that?

_____

_____

_____

3. Practice the Exchange Principle

To develop patience, you need to appreciate how other people think and be sensitive to how they feel. Every person thinks . . .

- His problems are biggest.
- His jokes are the funniest.
- His prayers should get special attention.
- His situation is different.
- His victories are the most exemplary.
- His faults should be overlooked.

In other words, each of us thinks our circumstances warrant special consideration—people should be extra patient with us. Instead, we should turn the tables: we should put ourselves in the other person's place (as I explained in the Exchange Principle), and be extra patient with them.

The next time you're feeling impatient with someone who is slowing you down, think about this story: a young woman's car stalled at a stoplight. She tried and tried to get it started, but had no luck whatsoever. The light turned green, and there she sat, angry and embarrassed, holding up traffic. The car behind her could have gone around, but instead the driver added to her frustration by laying on his horn.

After another desperate attempt to get the car started, she got out and walked back to the other car. The man rolled down his window in surprise.

"Tell you what," she said. "You go start my car, and I'll sit back here and honk the horn for you."

4. Realize that People *Have* and *Create* Problems

When it comes to people, there is good news and bad news. The good news is that some people in your life are going to be the source of your greatest joy. The bad news is that those same people may be the cause of your greatest problems. That's true not only at home but also at work. And the higher you climb in leadership, the more difficult the problems. The findings of leadership experts Warren Bennis and Burt Nanus bear this out. They state, "What we have found is that the higher the rank, the more interpersonal and human the undertaking. Our top executives spend roughly 90 percent of their time with others and virtually the same amount of time concerned with the messiness of people problems."[2]

When you decide to develop a relationship with another person, keep in mind that it's a package deal. You don't get to take only the good stuff and reject the bad. Everybody has problems, blind spots, and bad habits. Try to give others the same kind of grace you'd like to receive for your shortcomings.

5. Identify Areas Where People Need Patience with You

While we're on the subject of shortcomings, it's a good idea for us to know what *ours* are. For example, I know that the people closest to me need patience to put up with my idiosyncrasies. Ironically the first one is putting up with my impatience! (I'm working on that one.) But there are plenty of others. Just for fun, I asked my assistant, Linda Eggers, to give me a list of the areas where she has been longsuffering. It didn't take her long. Here are the top things she mentioned:

- I am constantly losing my cell phone and glasses.
- Any time we're discussing planning, I want lots of options.
- I am constantly changing my travel plans and needs.
- I overschedule myself, and as a result, projects take longer than the time allotted.
- I hate to say no.
- I want to be able to call her twenty-four hours a day, seven days a week.

I'm sure there are lots more, but that's enough. If I can keep in mind that others are being patient with me in multiple areas, it helps me to remember to be patient with others. Doing that may have a similar effect on you.

6. Recognize that All Relationships Have Give-Ups, Give-Ins, and Give-and-Takes

All relationships have difficult times. It doesn't matter how good they are or how long they've lasted. And we can't always have everything our own way. We will experience areas where we have to give:

- *There will be give-ups.* There will be things I like to do but should not do at this time. For example, when my children were small, I gave up golf. The game was just too time-consuming. My relationship with them was more important.

- *There will be give-ins.* There will be things I don't like to do but should do at this time. I don't particularly like to exercise, but I do want to spend more time on earth with my family and friends. So I get on the treadmill almost every day.

- *There will be give-and-takes.* There will be things we do for one another at this time. I remember one time that Margaret had gone to a women's retreat, and she called me because she wished she was at home. After I hung up the phone, I decided to surprise her by picking her up. It was a two-hour drive each way, but the trip was worth it.

What have you given up, given into, or seen as a give-and-take in your relationships?

_____

_____

_____

I should mention that nobody can make you give up, give in, or give and take. They are voluntary activities. But if you want relationships to last, you've got to be flexible. Take the advice of psychologist Joyce Brothers, who says that relationships should follow one of the rules of watercraft: "The more maneuverable boat should give way to the less flexible craft."

APPLYING THE PATIENCE PRINCIPLE

1. Are there particular personality types that are prone to impatience with other people? If so, describe them. Are there certain types who are especially slow? How can these two types learn to interact more positively?

_____

_____

_____

2. Think about the three to five people who are closest to you. How long have you known them? How did your relationships start? When you first met them, did you expect them to become close friends? How intentional was your investment in the relationship? How much time did it take to develop a deeper relationship? Could you have sped up the process, or did it require all of the time spent?

_____

_____

_____

3. What kinds of situations make people impatient with others? What particular situations make you impatient with people? How does that work against you in relationships? How can you change your attitude or actions to make you less impatient and better able to stay connected with others?

_____

_____

_____

4. In what kinds of relationships is it most difficult to give up what you want, give in to what the other person wants, and give and take in order to do what's best for the relationship? Where do goals come into play? How about values? In what situations would it be wrong to give up or give in? What is an appropriate balance of give-and-take? How can you make sure the relationship does not become unbalanced?

_____

_____

_____

5. Which of your quirks, idiosyncrasies, or oddities might cause others to have to be patient with you? (If you think you don't have any, talk to three close friends or family members, and ask them to tell you what they are.) Why should people be patient with you in these areas? Do you *expect* others to be patient and take it for granted, or are you grateful for their patience? Explain.

_____

_____

_____

Summary

Here's the bottom line when it comes to the Patience Principle. If you travel alone, you can probably go faster. But the journey will never be as rewarding, and you probably won't be able to go as far. With some people, we are patient with them because of the relationship. With other people, we are patient with them because of the return. And with still others, we are patient with them because of both. Every relationship requires patience, but in the end, it's worth it.

THE CELEBRATION PRINCIPLE

THE TRUE TEST OF RELATIONSHIPS IS NOT ONLY HOW LOYAL WE ARE WHEN FRIENDS FAIL, BUT HOW THRILLED WE ARE WHEN THEY SUCCEED

Average people do not want others to go beyond average.

THE QUESTION I MUST ASK MYSELF:
DO I ENJOY AND ROOT FOR
THE SUCCESS OF MY FRIENDS?

I believe in all the People Principles, and I work at practicing them every day of my life. But the Celebration Principle is especially important to me personally. I was very fortunate early in my career. I've known since I was four years old what I wanted to do in life. And I grew up in a home with a father who was experienced and successful in the profession in which I would follow him. The situation is similar to that of the Manning family in football. Successful NFL quarterback Peyton Manning (and his younger brother Eli) grew up in the home of Archie Manning, who played for the New Orleans Saints. As a result, they had a jump-start in football that 99 percent of other kids didn't.

In addition to the experiences and exposure I received from just being around my father, I benefited from his strong leadership. He was very strategic in my development, identifying and encouraging my strengths early. He sent me to several Dale Carnegie seminars before I graduated from high school, directed my growth through extensive reading, and took me to see and meet some of the great preachers of the era. The advantages I received are too many to list. I am truly grateful for all of them.

The result of my upbringing was that I saw success early in my career. I achieved a lot of firsts in my denomination. I was the youngest person to be elected to a national office. I was the first pastor to change the name of the church to better reach the community. I was the youngest to write his first book. And I had the first church that averaged more than one thousand in attendance every Sunday.

Unfortunately during those early years, I might have also been the loneliest pastor in my denomination. The good news was that when I failed, plenty of people were glad to commiserate with me. But when I succeeded, few celebrated. I thought my colleagues and I were on the same team, but evidently they didn't see it that way. Many times Margaret and I celebrated alone.

Do you find that people are more willing to console, you or to congratulate you? Explain.

_____

_____

_____

What I Learned
about the Celebration Principle

Those early experiences taught Margaret and me a lot. Many of the lessons we learned are things that you may also find valuable:

The Joy of the Accomplishment Is Diminished
When No One Celebrates with You

When I went to my denomination's conference following my first year as a pastor, I was excited about the things that were happening in my church. I was helping people, and I thought I was really making a difference in my community. My enthusiasm was unbounded. Much to my surprise, nobody shared my excitement! People seemed to look at me with skepticism or disdain. It really deflated me emotionally. The words of playwright Oscar Wilde were true: "Anybody can sympathize with the sufferings of a friend, but it requires a very fine nature to sympathize with a friend's success."

After Margaret and I talked about it, we decided that we would never let others' lack of enthusiasm hinder our own. And we also became determined to celebrate with friends when they succeeded—and to be even more enthusiastic when they surpassed us!

That's one reason I love doing conferences for young leaders. It gives me a chance to celebrate with them—and to champion their successes. I want them to feel encouraged and keep pursuing their dreams. There's no telling what they might accomplish with the knowledge that others want them to succeed.

How do you help to celebrate the accomplishments of others? With whom do you often celebrate?

_____

_____

_____

Many People Identify with Failure; Fewer People Identify with Success

Several years ago, I wrote a book called *Failing Forward*. As I was preparing to work on it, I lectured on the subject around the country. And what I found was that *everyone* identifies with failure. In fact, when I told people that they needed to learn how to use their mistakes as stepping-stones for success by *failing forward*, the reaction of the audience was audible. They wanted to learn how to fail forward.

What I've discovered over the years of working with people is the following: you may be able to impress people with your successes, but if you want to influence them, share your failures. Everybody has failed, so it's a great way to connect.

The problem is that because people so readily identify with failure, they sometimes have a hard time connecting with success. And if they don't identify with success, they may resent it.

Have you ever been reluctant to celebrate a friend or colleague's success? Why?

_____

_____

_____

What Hinders People from Success Often Keeps Them from Celebrating Others' Success

Frequently the very same qualities that prevent people from achieving success—emotional insecurity, a scarcity mind-set, petty jealousy, etc.—prevent them from celebrating others' successes. They constantly compare themselves to others and find themselves wanting. As a result, they have a hard time getting beyond themselves.

Professional speaker Joe Larson once said, "My friends didn't believe that I could become a successful speaker. So I did something about it. I went out and found me some new friends!" It's sad, but sometimes that's what it takes.

Do you feel that there is only so much praise or recognition to go around? Explain.

_____

_____

_____

The People Who Celebrate with You Become Lifelong Friends

Back during the first years of my career, two people outside my family who celebrated with us when we succeeded were Dave and Mary Vaughn. Dave was a few years ahead of me in his career, and he was always ready to cheer me on when I achieved a goal or passed a milestone. Even when my church grew to be larger than his and I gained more notoriety, he never held back. And thirty-five years later, he and Mary still celebrate with us!

BEWARE OF THE GREEN-EYED MONSTER

In October 2003 at *Catalyst*, a conference for young leaders put on by one of my companies, Andy Stanley spoke at a session. Andy is an effective and authentic communicator. He leads Northpoint Community Church, one of the top churches in the country with an attendance of more than fifteen thousand people every weekend. (Just in case you are unfamiliar with the church world, that puts Northpoint in the top 1 percent of all churches in America.)

Andy's second session was about four negative characteristics that can trip up a leader: guilt, anger, greed, and jealousy. Andy confessed that he sometimes experiences moments of professional jealousy when hearing other successful people speak. He said, "I have to make an extra effort to celebrate the success of other people who do what I do."

That potential for jealousy extends even to Andy's closest friends, including Louie Giglio, who sometimes speaks at Andy's church. Andy explained,

> Louie and I have been friends since the sixth grade . . . We met at youth camp under a bunk bed while seniors battled it out above our heads. Louie is just a phenomenal communicator. When I announce at our church that Louie Giglio is going to be speaking next week, they all start clapping and we have high attendance Sunday. And then for four or five days the rest of the week everyone's going, "Oh, Louie, Louie, Louie."

Andy went on to tell how Louie always teaches to capacity crowds at his events and delivers outstanding material. And every time Andy hears him speak, tiny pangs of jealousy threaten to rear their ugly heads.

Such feelings could destroy Andy and Louie's relationship, and that relationship is deep. Not only do they work together, but their families are close, and they even go on vacations together. How does Andy handle the envy he feels? By celebrating Louie's accomplishments. When Louie delivers a great message, Andy goes out of his way to praise him and celebrate with him. And Louie does the same with him. Andy said, "It's not enough to think it. I have to say it because that's how I cleanse my heart. Celebration is how you defeat jealousy."

BECOMING A PARTY STARTER

Andy isn't alone. If most people were honest, they would admit to feelings of jealousy or envy when they witness others' success—even when the people succeeding are close friends.

I know I've fought feelings of jealousy. Haven't you? So how do you learn to celebrate with others instead of ignoring or undermining them? Start by doing these four things:

1. Realize It's Not a Competition

It's impossible to do anything of real significance on your own. It's very difficult to achieve success without help. And even if you do become successful, you won't enjoy it without friends. Life is better in a community of people you love and who also love you.

When I reflect on the value of community, many thoughts come to mind:

> *My success can be achieved only with others.*
> *My lessons can be learned only from others.*
> *My weaknesses can be strengthened only by others.*
> *My servanthood can be tested only under others' leadership.*
> *My influence can be compounded only through others.*
> *My leadership can be focused only on others.*
> *My best can be given only to others.*
> *My legacy can be left only for others.*
> *So I should commit myself to and celebrate with others!*

Other people have an impact on every aspect of life. Most of the time, I choose with my attitude whether that impact is positive or negative.

Think about your greatest successes. Who helped you to achieve those successes?

_____

_____

_____

2. Celebrate When They See Success

Not everyone views success the way you do. When it comes to the Celebration Principle, you must be willing to look at things from other people's point of view. What are their dreams? What goals have they set? What battles are they fighting? When they achieve something that is important to *them*, then celebrate! And be especially careful when a friend accomplishes something that you've already achieved and perhaps find to be old hat. Be sure to celebrate with enthusiasm. Never steal another person's thunder.

3. Celebrate Successes They Don't Yet See

Sometimes people make great strides and aren't even aware of it. Have you ever started to diet or exercise and after a while felt that you were struggling, only to have a friend tell you how good you look? Or haven't you worked on a project and felt discouraged by your progress, but had a friend marvel at what you had accomplished? It is inspiring and makes you want to work that much harder. If you *haven't* had a friend do that for you, then you may need some new friends—people who practice the Celebration Principle.

Who around you is working on a goal? How can you encourage that person?

_____

_____

_____

4. Celebrate Most with Those Closest to You

The closer people are to you and the more important the relationship, the more you ought to celebrate. Celebrate early and often with those closest to you—especially with your spouse and children if you have a family. It's usually easy to celebrate victories on the job or in a hobby or sport. But the greatest victories in life are the ones that occur at home.

My friend Dan Reiland says, "A genuine friend encourages and challenges us to live out our best thoughts, honor our purest motives, and achieve our most significant dreams." That's what we need to do with the important people in our lives.

APPLYING THE CELEBRATION PRINCIPLE

1. Do you agree that most people more readily identify with failure than with success? Explain your answer. What do the people who identify with success possess that others don't? Do they still need the encouragement that comes with friends' celebrating their successes? Why?

_____

_____

_____

2. Some people have trouble celebrating even their own accomplishments. Why is that? How are you when it comes to celebrating successes? Do you take time to celebrate the achievement of milestones and goals? If not, why not? If you don't acknowledge your achievements, will you be enthusiastic about celebrating those of others? What must you do to change your attitude toward yourself and others? If you do celebrate your victories and achievements, how much is too much? Why?

_____

_____

_____

3. Who celebrates with you? Do you have friends, colleagues, or family members who cheer you on? If the answer is no, then you need to cultivate new friendships with people who are more encouraging and who focus on your strengths. If the answer is yes, thank them for their support and be sure to celebrate with them.

_____

_____

_____

4. Which is your natural bent: to engage in competition or to foster cooperation? Can people be competitive and still practice the Celebration Principle effectively? Can people be cooperative by nature, yet neglect to celebrate with others? Explain. What things can people do to foster a celebratory spirit in themselves, regardless of their personality type?

_____

_____

_____

5. Think of people you go out of your way to celebrate with. Are there other people in your life who would be especially encouraged and lifted up by celebration on your part? For whom in your life is it your _responsibility_ to encourage through celebration? What would you like to start doing differently to help others celebrate?

_____

_____

_____

Summary

The journey is a lot more fun if you take somebody with you. You can't do that if your success is the only thing you celebrate. If you want others to succeed alongside you, then you must encourage them and celebrate their successes. Not only does it give them the incentive to keep striving for their dreams, but it also helps them enjoy the journey along the way. As I began reaching out and celebrating others' successes, I found that the success of others brought me more joy than my success.

Entertainer Bette Midler said, "The worst part of success is trying to find someone who is happy for you." Don't look at your friends, family, and teammates as competition. Be the rare kind of person who is happy when others succeed.

THE HIGH ROAD PRINCIPLE

WE GO TO A HIGHER LEVEL WHEN WE TREAT OTHERS BETTER than THEY TREAT US

Keep a fair-sized cemetery in your back yard,
in which to bury the faults of your friends.

—HENRY WARD BEECHER

THE QUESTION I MUST ASK MYSELF:
DO I TREAT OTHERS BETTER
THAN THEY TREAT ME?

In 1842, thirteen-year-old William Booth's life changed. His father, Samuel Booth, lost his business. The elder Booth had once been a nail maker, but when his trade became the victim of mass production, he started a business as a small-time builder. Unfortunately, recurring recessions had taken their toll, and finally Booth went out of business. It put him and his family into difficult circumstances. As a result, William, who had grown up in a household with enough money to have him educated, was sent out to learn a trade. He was apprenticed to a pawnbroker in a seedy part of Nottingham, England.

"Make money" was the advice of Booth's father, who died bankrupt the next year. Booth did learn about making money while learning his trade. But his apprenticeship also gave him another kind of education. Working in a pawnbroker's shop, he was in daily contact with the poor and destitute. One biography noted, "He learned as from a primer what poverty did to people."[1] It's no coincidence that during his years as an apprentice, he became a person of faith—a Christian.

A CHANGE OF HEART

In 1849, Booth moved to London and took a position in a pawn shop in a poor area south of the Thames River. But after only three years, he gave up this trade and became a minister. He saw faith as the solution to the problems of those who were struggling to survive. And he embarked on a lifelong mission that had two objectives: saving lost souls and righting social injustices.[2]

At first he became a Methodist New Connexion minister, then a traveling evangelist. But in 1865 when some people from the area heard him preach in front of the Blind Beggar Pub in East London, he was recruited to become part of a tent ministry that came to be called the Christian Mission.

From there, Booth ministered to the poorest people in London. The East End contained half of the paupers, homeless, and starving in London.[3] His early converts were some of the most desperate types of people: thieves, prostitutes, gamblers, and drunkards.

He was trying to make a difference, but his efforts were not met with appreciation, including from the very people he was trying to help.

He and his fellow workers were harassed and brutalized. Local tavern keepers worked especially hard to undermine his efforts. Even street children threw stones and fireworks through the windows of their meeting hall. Catherine Booth, wife of William Booth, said that he would "stumble home night after night, haggard with fatigue. Often his clothes were torn and bloody, bandages swathed his head where a stone had struck."[4] But Booth would not retaliate in kind. And he refused to give up.

Booth worked to feed the poor, house the homeless, and share his faith. His organization continued to grow. By 1867, he had ten full-time workers. By 1874, more than one thousand volunteers and forty-two evangelists worked with him. In 1878 when they reorganized, Booth gave the group a new name. From then on, the organization would be called the Salvation Army.

Unfortunately that didn't stop the group's opponents. Booth was labeled "anti-Christ" by the reformer Lord Shaftesbury.[5] An opposition group formed to try to stop Booth and his associates. They came to call themselves the Skeleton Army. An article in the *Bethnal Green Eastern Post* in November 1882 described them:

> A genuine rabble of "roughs" pure and unadulterated has been infesting the district for several weeks past. These vagabonds style themselves the "Skeleton Army" . . . The object of the Skeleton Army was to put down the Salvationists by following them about everywhere, by beating a drum and burlesquing their songs, to render the conduct of their processions and services impossible . . . Amongst the skeleton rabble there is a large percentage of . . . loafers and unmitigated blackguards . . . [and] the disreputable class of publicans who hate the London school board, education and temperance, and who, seeing the beginning of the end of their immoral trafic [*sic*], and prepared for the most desparate [*sic*] enterprise.[6]

Despite the horrible treatment they received, the officers and volunteers in the Salvation Army persevered, and they helped hundreds of thousands of people.[7] Often, they converted the very individuals who had persecuted them.

In 1912, William Booth, then age eighty-three, delivered his last public address. In it he stated his commitment to investing in people:

While women weep as they do now, I'll fight; while little children go hungry as they do now, I'll fight; while men go to prison, in and out, in and out, as they do now, I'll fight; while there is a drunkard left, while there is a poor lost girl on the streets, while there remains one dark soul without the light of God, I'll fight—I'll fight to the very end.[8]

Three months later, he died. As one observer put it, the "general" who had led the Salvation Army for more than thirty years was "promoted to glory."

Who do you admire that follows the High Road Principle? In what ways has he or she taken the high road?

_____

_____

_____

William Booth spent a lifetime practicing the High Road Principle. He continually treated others better than they treated him. And as a result, he lived on the highest level, personally and professionally. I greatly admire William Booth, but I must say I didn't always believe in the High Road Principle. When I was a teenager, my father, Melvin Maxwell, was the president of a Bible college. I often watched in frustration as the college's board of directors was difficult to work with and treated him poorly. Yet no matter how the directors treated him, my father never retaliated; he always took the high road. At the time, his response made me furious.

As I got older and worked with more difficult people, I better understood my father's actions. I realized that if you're slinging mud, you're losing ground. There are really only three roads we can travel when it comes to dealing with others. We can take . . .

> the low road—where we treat others worse than they treat us.
> the middle road—where we treat others the same as they treat us.
> the high road—where we treat others better than they threat us.

The low road damages relationships and alienates others from us. The middle road may not drive people away from us, but it won't attract them to us either; it is reactive rather than proactive and allows others to set the agenda for our lives. The high road helps to create positive relationships and attracts others to us; it sets a positive agenda with others that even negative people find difficult to undermine. Taking the cue from my father, I decided to work at taking the high road with others every day.

What do you think it means to follow the high road every day?

_____

_____

_____

HIGH ROAD TRAVELERS

The high road truly is the path less traveled. I say that because taking the high road requires thinking and acting in ways that are not natural or common. However, those who practice the High Road Principle become instruments of grace to others and recipients of grace. And I've observed that "high roaders" have several things in common:

High Roaders Understand that It's Not What Happens *to* You but What Happens *in* You that Really Matters

During the Civil War, Confederate General W. H. C. Whiting was jealous of rival general Robert E. Lee. Consequently Whiting spread many rumors about him. But there came a time when General Lee could have gotten even. When President Jefferson Davis was considering Whiting for a key promotion, he asked General Lee what he thought of Whiting. Without hesitation, Lee endorsed and commended Whiting. The other officers who witnessed the exchange were astonished. Afterward, one of them asked Lee if he had forgotten all the unkind words that Whiting had spread about him.

"I understand that the president wanted to know my opinion of Whiting," responded Lee, "not Whiting's opinion of me."

Newscaster David Brinkley observed, "A successful man is one who can lay a firm foundation with the bricks others have thrown at him." That's what high road travelers do. They stay true to their core values and treat people according to them, not according to external circumstances.

What happens when you react based on external circumstances?

_____

_____

_____

High Roaders Commit Themselves to Traveling the High Road Continually

Nearly anyone can be kind in the face of unkindness every once in a while. It's more difficult to sustain a high road attitude all the time. Hector LeMarque remarked, "Most people make some good choices every day, but they don't make enough good choices to create momentum and obtain success." That's a good insight on what happens for people who take the high road all the time: they create momentum. They also cultivate relational success. Why? Because responding best today puts them in the best place tomorrow.

How does taking the high road today put us in the best position for tomorrow? Give an example from your own life.

High Roaders See Their Own Need for Grace, and Therefore, They Extend It to Others

One of the most dramatic stories I've ever read illustrating the high road spirit came from the life of Corrie ten Boom, author of *The Hiding Place*. She and her family worked with the underground and hid Jews from the Nazis in their home during World War II. When their actions were discovered, they were arrested by the Gestapo and sent to the Ravensbruck death camp. Every one of her family members died, and only because of a paperwork error did she survive and obtain her release.

A strong woman of faith, ten Boom lectured often after the war. In 1947, she returned to Ravensbruck to speak about God's grace and forgiveness to the German people. After she spoke, she found herself face-to-face with the cruelest guard she had encountered at Ravensbruck.

"It could not have been many seconds that he stood there—hand held out," she wrote, "but to me it seemed hours as I wrestled with the most difficult thing I ever had to do." Finally she extended her hand and forgave him. She took the most difficult of all high roads.

Is there an injustice that you have not been willing to forgive? Who does your unforgiveness affect the most? How would things be different if you chose to forgive this person or group?

_____

_____

_____

High Roaders Are Not Victims; They Choose to Serve Others

People who take the high road don't do so because no other roads are open to them. They do it as an act of will according to a desire to serve others. They are like the grandmother at her golden wedding anniversary celebration who told the guests the secret of her happy marriage. "On my wedding day," she said, "I decided to make a list of ten of my husband's faults that, for the sake of our marriage, I would overlook." As the guests were leaving, a young wife asked the older woman to name some of the faults that she had overlooked.

"To tell you the truth," the grandmother said, "I never did get around to making the list. But whenever my husband did something that made me hopping mad, I would say to myself, 'Lucky for him that's one of the ten!'" Because the high road is uphill, no one travels it by accident.

High Roaders Set Higher Standards for Themselves than Others Would

James Michener, the author of *Tales of the South Pacific, Texas, Centennial, Space,* and many other novels, was a prolific writer who gained respect for his literary prowess and sales success. However, he always had one detractor who remained a thorn in his side for years.

Abandoned as an infant, the author never knew his biological parents. Fortunately he was taken in and raised as a foster son by a widow. He became a Michener, adopting the name of his new family. But each time he published a new book, he received nasty notes from one of the Michener clan. The relative chastised him for besmirching the good Michener name—despite the fact the writer won a Pulitzer Prize—which he said the novelist had no right to use.

Despite the berating, Michener did agree with one thing the relative said. The novelist particularly remembered the comment: "Who do you think you are, trying to be better than you are?" Michener said. "I've spent my life trying to be better than I was, and I am a brother to all who share the same aspiration."

People who embrace the high road make excellence their goal. That's something that can be accomplished if we . . .

Care more than others think is wise.
Risk more than others think is safe.
Dream more than others think is practical.
Expect more than others think is possible.
Work more than others think is necessary.

When we conduct ourselves according to our highest standards, we are less likely to be defensive and take the low road when attacked by others. I say that because when you know you've done all you can do, you can let criticism roll off your back like rain.

How do you feel before you take the high road? How does it make you feel after you do take the high road?

_____

_____

_____

High Roaders Bring Out the Best in Others

Have you ever heard the fable of the lion and the skunk? A proud, loud, and especially obnoxious skunk challenged a lion to a fight. The lion promptly and emphatically declined the challenge.

"Hah!" sneered the skunk. "You're afraid to fight me!"

"No," answered the lion, "but why should I fight you? You would gain fame from fighting me, even though I gave you the worst beating of your life—which I would do. But how about me? I couldn't possibly gain anything by defeating you. On the other hand, everyone I met for a month would know that I had been in the company of a skunk."

The high road is the only path that brings out the best in others. Philosopher-poet Johann Wolfgang von Goethe advised, "Treat people as though they were what they ought to be and you will help them become what they are capable of becoming."

Do you agree with Wolfgang von Goethe that people tend to live up to or down to your expectations of them? Explain.

_____

_____

_____

High Roaders Bring Out the Best in Themselves

Making it your practice to always treat others the best that you can affects the way you see the world—and yourself. President Abraham Lincoln said, "Die when I may, I want it said of me by those who knew me best that I always plucked a thistle and planted a flower where I thought a flower would grow." That is what the High Road Principle does to a person's heart over the course of time: it plants flowers where thorny weeds once thrived. The way that you treat others is your statement to the world of who you are. Are you making the kind of statement you desire?

If you don't already practice the High Road Principle, I hope you will embrace it from this day forward. It is probably the best investment you can make in a relationship. If you need a little help moving to the high road, then follow these "directions":

1. Stay on Kindness Street as long as possible.

2. Turn right on Forgiveness Avenue.

3. Avoid Get Even Alley because it is a dead end.

4. Climb to the top of the hill, for there you will see the high road.

5. Take it and stay on it; and if you lose your way, ask God for help.

The high road is often not the easiest road, but it is the only one that leads to the highest level of living.

APPLYING THE HIGH ROAD PRINCIPLE

1. How would you define the *high road*? Why is it difficult to take the high road with someone who is taking the low road with you? What particular low road actions by others do you find difficult to overcome or ignore?

_____

_____

_____

2. Why do most people take the middle road? How does that affect their relationships? Can a person stay on the middle road and still be an investor in people? Explain.

_____

_____

_____

3. What happens to relationships when people have a get-even mind-set? Can a person desire revenge in one area of life without it affecting other relationships? What does harboring the desire for revenge do to a person emotionally, physically, and spiritually?

_____

_____

_____

4. Describe a difficult situation where you chose to take the high road in a relationship. Why was it difficult? How were you able to overcome your desire to respond in kind? Is that a strategy you use effectively very often? Where did you learn it, or how did you develop it?

_____

_____

_____

Summary

I once saw a sign that read, "To err is human, to forgive—is not company policy." It's funny, but it also hints at people's natural inclination not to give individuals a break when they act in a way that shows their human frailty. Let's face it. We're all human and make mistakes. People who take the high road recognize their humanness, know that they need to be extended grace, and are accordingly more likely to extend it to others.

THE SYNERGY QUESTION
CAN WE CREATE A WIN-WIN
RELATIONSHIP?

*Win/Win is a frame of mind and heart that constantly seeks mutual bene-
fit in all human interactions . . . Win/Win is based on the paradigm that
there is plenty for everybody, that one person's success is not achieved at the
expense or exclusion of the success of others.*

—STEPHEN R. COVEY

I f we're honest about relationships, we'll admit that there are some people with whom
we want to spend time, and others with whom we don't. What separates the good relationships we desire from the ones that don't do anything for us? The answer is synergy.
Some relationships are a win-win. They add value to both parties, and that is rewarding.

I believe that every relationship has the *potential* to be win-win, though not all relationships achieve that quality. But when both parties enter into a relationship with an
investment mind-set—after having connected and built trust with each other—a win-
win relationship is often the result.

The wonderful thing about win-win relationships is that they can be forged in every
area of life and in all kinds of relationships: between husbands and wives, parents and
children, friends and neighbors, bosses and employees. If both parties sustain a giving

attitude and both are having their needs met, then the relationship can become something truly special. The "currency" that they give each other doesn't have to be the same. They may provide each other unconditional love. Or one person may provide loyal admiration, and the other security. One may provide mentoring, and the other gratitude. One may build the business, and the other may provide a paycheck. One may provide humor, and the other may be a great audience. As long as both people experience consistent wins in areas they value, they develop synergy.

The following People Principles answer the question, "Can we create a win-win relationship?" and will help anyone who practices them create relationships with synergy.

The Boomerang Principle: When we help others, we help ourselves.

The Friendship Principle: All things being equal, people will work with people they like; all things not being equal, they still will.

The Partnership Principle: Working together increases the odds of winning together.

The Satisfaction Principle: In great relationships, the joy of being together is enough.

In the long run, lopsided relationships don't last. If one person is doing all the giving and the other is doing all the receiving, the giver will eventually become worn out. And ironically the taker will become dissatisfied because he will feel he is not receiving enough. The only way to build a positive, long-lasting, synergistic relationship is to make sure everybody wins!

THE BOOMERANG PRINCIPLE

WHEN WE HELP OTHERS, WE HELP OURSELVES

No man becomes rich unless he enriches others.

—ANDREW CARNEGIE

THE QUESTION I MUST ASK MYSELF:
DO I EXPERIENCE A RETURN
WHEN I HELP OTHERS?

I n the early years of my career, I did not have a correct view of life. I approached life like it was a slot machine. I wanted to put as little as possible into it, and I always hoped to hit the jackpot. I'm embarrassed to say that I often had a similar approach in my interaction with people. I was more focused on what people could do for me than what I could do for them. As a result, I would try to make relational "withdrawals" without ever having made any "deposits." Needless to say, I was not very successful.

As I spent more time working with others, my thinking slowly began to change. I began to learn the Big Picture Principle, to see people in a different light, and to place a higher value on them. Once my attitude started changing, so did my actions. I started to invest in people simply because they had value. They were important. And I found that when I focused on what I could give rather than what I could get, people blossomed, relationships matured, and life was more rewarding. After I started to make giving my goal, I often felt that I received more from people than I was able to give.

Over the course of many years, I began learning to invest in people first and often. Somebody has to make the first move in relationships. So I figured, *Why not me?* I started to take a giver's approach to life, focusing on what I could give in relationships. And I often tried to do it without an expectation of receiving something in return. I discovered that when I added value to people, many desired to add value back to me. When that happened, the relationships developed an incredible synergy and went to a new level.

When you meet someone, which is more likely to be your first thought:
1) what can this person do for me, or 2) how can I help this person? Why?

_____

_____

_____

WHAT GOES AROUND . . .

Where do you stand on the subject of giving to others? I believe there are only three kinds of people when it comes to this subject:

1. *Takers receive and never give.* Many people focus on themselves and rarely go out of their way to do anything for others. Such people are takers. They worry only about what they can get, and they are never satisfied.

2. *Traders receive and then give.* Some people focus on keeping score. They are willing to give, but their primary motivation isn't to help others. They see relationships as an exchange. Often they give because they think they owe something to someone who has helped them, and they desire to make things "even." I was like that early in my career. I was grateful to people who helped me, but I didn't understand the value of adding value to others. And I didn't initiate giving.

3. *Investors give and then receive.* In this third group, people focus on others. They give first and then receive if something is offered in return. They believe that success comes from being helpful, caring, and constructive. They desire to make everything and everyone they touch better, and they understand that the best way to accomplish that is to give of themselves. Ironically, by possessing an agenda to give first, they are the ones who most often experience the synergy of win-win relationships.

At what points in your life have you been a taker, a trader, and an investor?

_____

_____

_____

People who invest in other people have some things in common:

Investors Understand that People Are of Great Value

Once when I was speaking to employees at Bell South telephone company, an executive for the company stated, "People are our company's most appreciable asset." I heard good news and bad news in that statement. The good news is that he truly valued his people and cared about their well-being. The bad news is that what he said is only partly true. People are an *appreciating* asset only if we are willing to *invest* in them. Most people, if left alone, remain much the same.

Are you involved in an organization that invests in people? How does that affect your involvement and belief in that organization?

_____

_____

_____

Investors Embrace the Boomerang Principle

People who invest in others know that the best way to help themselves is to help others. They start that investment process by investing in relationships. They see everyone as a potential friend. Counselor and author Alan Loy McGinnis noted,

> In research at our clinic, my colleagues and I have discovered that friendship is the springboard to every other love. Friendships spill over onto the other important relationships of life. People with no friends usually have a diminished capacity for sustaining any kind of love. They tend to go through a succession of marriages, be estranged from various family members, and have trouble getting along at work. On the other hand, those who learn how to love their friends tend to make long and fulfilling marriages, get along well with the people at work, and enjoy their children.[1]

When you invest in a friendship, you open the door to investment—and ultimately the possibility of a return.

Should all your friendships be win-win relationships? Explain.

_____

_____

_____

Investors Practice the Principle of Sowing and Reaping

There has never been a person who gave that did not receive in return! You may not believe that, but it is a fact. The Boomerang Principle is true: when we help others, we help ourselves. Here's why I say that. Whenever you give to another person, you will receive something in return that affects your valuables, your values, or your virtues.

- _Valuables: the things that provide financial worth._ When people think about receiving something in return for giving, their thoughts often turn to material benefits. Sometimes when you help others, you do receive something of financial worth. But that is only one kind of benefit and perhaps not the most common kind.

- *Values: the things that bring fulfillment.* Have you ever given anonymously? If so, then you understand that while you received nothing tangible in return, you benefited emotionally or spiritually. Anytime you do something to fulfill your values, you benefit.

- *Virtues: the things that develop character.* Many benefits we receive from giving come in the area of character. Every time you overcome the inclination to be greedy by giving, you become less selfish. Every time you help someone and don't see an immediate return, you become more patient. Such things build character.

In nature, if you sow, you reap. What you reap depends on what you plant. And you always reap later than you sow. The same is true when it comes to relationships. As in nature, they take time.

Give examples of how your investment in others has affected your valuables, values, and virtues.

_____

_____

_____

Investors Believe that Helping Others Is the Divine Work of People

American literary giant Ralph Waldo Emerson advised,

Don't be a cynic . . . [and] bewail and bemoan. Omit the negative propositions . . . Don't waste yourself in rejection, nor bark against the bad, but chant the beauty of the good . . . Set down nothing that will not help somebody. It is one of the beautiful compensations of life that no man can sincerely try to help another without helping himself. To help the young soul, to add energy, inspire hope, and blow the coals into a useful flame; to redeem defeat by new thought and firm action: This, though not easy, is the work of divine man.

TAKE INVESTING IN OTHERS TO A NEW LEVEL

Investing in others is one of the most noble and productive things we can do. Whatever we can do to help others makes the world a better place. As President Woodrow Wilson said, "You are not here merely to make a living. You are here in order to enable the world to live more amply, with greater vision, with a finer spirit of hope and achievement. You are here to enrich the world, and you impoverish yourself if you forget the errand."

So how do you enrich the world and become someone who invests in others? Begin by taking these five steps:

1. Think "Others First"

It was with good reason that I began this book with the Big Picture Principle. Good, healthy, growing relationships begin with the ability to put other people first. Work to develop an attitude of kindness toward everyone. Begin every relationship by giving the other person respect—even before he has had a chance to earn it. Initiate acts of kindness with everyone.

How can you show that you respect a person when you first meet?

_____

_____

_____

2. Focus on the Investment, Not the Return

Novelist Herman Melville believed that "we cannot live only for ourselves. A thousand fibers connect us with our fellow men; and along those fibers, as sympathetic threads, our actions run as causes, and they come back to us as effects." We are intimately linked with other people, and our destinies are interwoven. As a result, when we help others, we will benefit. But that is not where we should place our focus.

Investors in people are like investors in the stock market. In the long haul, they will benefit, but they have little control over what that return will look like or how it will occur. But they *can* control what and how they invest. And that's where they should focus their time and energy.

What does it mean to focus on the investment and not the return?

_____

_____

_____

3. Pick Out a Few People with Great Potential

In 1995 when I began investing in people full-time, I felt called to invest strategically in ten people. My desire was to pick people with great potential and invest in them to help them become better leaders. The list of people has changed over the years, but my commitment to serving others has not. If anything, it has intensified. In 1995, I simply wanted to add value to others. Now ten years later, I want to multiply value to others by adding value to leaders.

When people prepare to make financial investments, the wise ones don't put all their money into a single stock or fund. They diversify by investing in several areas. (If you invest in only one and it doesn't perform well, you're in trouble.) But good investors don't spread themselves too thin, either. They know they can give only so much time and attention to each particular investment. Wise investors in people follow a similar pattern. Pick only as many people as you can handle with intensity, choose only people with great potential for growth, and choose only people whose need for growth matches your gifts and talents.

Taking into consideration the commitments you already have, how many people could you realistically invest in? How much time would you need to spend with each person?

_____

_____

_____

4. With Their Permission, Begin the Process

You cannot help someone who does not want your help. That seems so obvious that I hesitate to say it, but I feel that I must because I see people with good intentions trying to initiate the process without getting the buy-in of the person they're trying to help.

In *The 21 Irrefutable Laws of Leadership*, the Law of Buy-In says that people buy into the leader, then the vision. Mentoring relationships possess a leader-follower dynamic. The people being mentored must trust and believe in their teachers. The stronger the relationships and the greater the trust, the higher the likelihood that the investment process will work. But it must begin with agreement.

5. Enjoy a Return in Due Season

Poet Edwin Markham wrote,

> There is a destiny that marks us as brothers;
> No one goes his way alone:
> All that we send into the lives of others
> Comes back into our own.

APPLYING THE BOOMERANG PRINCIPLE

1. In the past, how have you approached relationships: as a taker, a trader, or an investor? If you have been a taker, why do you think you have been reluctant to give of yourself to others? If you have been a trader, in what ways have you "kept score" with other people? If you have been an investor, in what specific ways have you invested in others? Do you desire to change the way you see relationships? If so, why?

_____

_____

_____

2. Is it possible to add value to people if you don't value people? Explain your response. Describe the characteristics of someone who values people and puts others first. Think of someone you know who fits this profile. How do you measure up?

_____

_____

_____

3. How should one go about the process of selecting people to invest in? What traits should all people to be invested in possess? What specific needs or characteristics should a person you would mentor possess? Why?

_____

_____

_____

4. What are your greatest talents and gifts? Are these traits that can be shared? In what way can you use them to add value to others?

_____

_____

_____

5. What is your plan for intentionally investing in others? Do you have a process already in place? If so, how has it worked? What do you need to change? What have others done that might work for you? If you have not yet created a plan, what do you think it should include? Have you observed a model that works? If so, what parts of it will you embrace? When will you start?

_____

_____

_____

Summary

I am convinced that when people's motives are pure and they genuinely desire to add value to others, they cannot help others without receiving some benefit. The return may be immediate, or it may take a long time, but it will occur. And when it does, the relationship begins to resonate with synergy.

You are probably familiar with the story of Helen Keller, the deaf and blind girl whose life was transformed thanks to the efforts of Anne Sullivan. Keller, who was only seven when Sullivan came into her life, lived almost like an animal. But Sullivan taught her to communicate and opened the world to her. By the time Keller was an adult, she was able to take care of herself. She went on to receive a degree from Radcliffe College and to become a famous author and lecturer.

What you may not know is that when Anne Sullivan became ill years later, the person who took care of her was none other than Helen Keller. The helper became the one who needed help, and the one to whom she had added value turned around and added value to her. Invest in others, and like a boomerang, it will come back to you, sometimes in a most unexpected way.

THE FRIENDSHIP PRINCIPLE

ALL THINGS BEING EQUAL, PEOPLE WILL WORK WITH PEOPLE THEY LIKE; ALL THINGS NOT BEING EQUAL, THEY STILL WILL

The most I can do for my friend is simply be his friend.

—HENRY DAVID THOREAU

THE QUESTION I MUST ASK MYSELF:
AM I A FRIEND TO THE PEOPLE I WORK WITH?

If you were suddenly faced with a huge project that had a tough deadline and you needed to pull together a group of people to help you accomplish it, who would you ask for help? Would you enlist the aid of the people in your office who give you the most trouble? Would you go out of your way to partner with people who rub you the wrong way? Of course not!

What if you became aware of a business opportunity that you knew was the chance of a lifetime? How would you pursue it? Would you use the Yellow Pages to find people to help you? Would you put an ad in the newspaper looking for a business partner? Certainly not! You would mentally review the friends and associates qualified to help, and you would choose the people with whom you have the best relationships. And if two people had the same level of skill, you'd pick the person you most like to work with.

All that may seem painfully obvious to you as you read it. However, I believe that most people underestimate the power and importance of relationships in regard to business and career. They try to learn the most recent management fad. They focus on product quality. They create programs and systems to improve productivity or increase repeat business. They collect email addresses. These things may be helpful, but the real key is relationships. Never underestimate the power of friendship and likeability when it comes to doing business.

To see an excellent example of the Friendship Principle, look at the life of Bill Porter. If ever there was a person with obstacles to succeeding in business, he was it. Porter was born with cerebral palsy. As a child, he was always physically behind his peers. From birth, his right hand has been nearly useless, and verbal communication has always been difficult. The so-called experts thought he was retarded and advised his parents to institutionalize him. They refused. Instead they made major adjustments to their lifestyle, worked with him, and helped him to cultivate independence. Porter worked hard and completed high school, receiving his diploma.

DETERMINED TO MAKE IT

After high school, he looked for work with the aid of the Oregon Department of Employment. He took a job as a stock clerk and was fired after only one day. He worked as a cashier for Goodwill and lasted only three days. He took jobs at the Salvation Army working on the loading dock and at the Veterans Administration answering phones. After more firings, the department of employment deemed him "unemployable."

But Porter wouldn't give up. He didn't want to live his life accepting a government disability check. When he got an opportunity to sell household items to raise money for United Cerebral Palsy, he loved it. He decided to make sales his career. He had a hard time finding a company that would give him a try, though. Finally he persuaded the director of Watkins Incorporated to give him a chance. He was reluctantly offered a territory that no other salesman would accept—working for straight commission. Porter would be selling household products door-to-door.

That was in the 1950s. Today, Porter is in his seventies, and he still works for Watkins. For decades he got up in the morning at 5:45, took two hours to laboriously get ready and dressed, caught buses across town to his territory, and haltingly walked seven to ten miles every day, going door-to-door selling products such as vanilla, spices, and detergents. He won his first sales award more than forty years ago and long ago became Watkins' number one salesman in the Northwest. In an era when door-to-door salesmen faded away, he continued to thrive.

How did he do it? His first asset has always been persistence. His second has been friendship. How else could you explain the continued success of a salesman whom people find difficult to understand, selling products that can be bought cheaper at discount stores, being sold in a method that went out of style decades ago, from a man who asks his customers to complete their own order forms because he has trouble writing? As Shelly Brady, who has assisted Porter since she was seventeen, says, "He snuck into people's hearts."[1]

What factors determine where you will and will not shop or do business?

_____

_____

_____

THE FOUR LEVELS OF BUSINESS RELATIONSHIPS

As soon as you understand the way that relationships affect business, you begin to realize that all business relationships are not created equal. As I have studied the subject, I've found that there are four levels:

1. People Knowledge—Your Understanding of People Helps Build Your Business

In the introduction of this book, I discussed the importance of people skills in business relationships. They are absolutely essential to success. All the product knowledge in the world won't help someone without people skills. Nor will technical expertise. Nor will the ability to build a brilliantly efficient organization. If individuals don't possess people skills, they very quickly hit a ceiling in their effectiveness.

An interesting way that some people overcome a lack of expertise in people knowledge is to partner with someone who possesses it in abundance. For example, people like Steve Wozniak and Steve Jobs brought together technical skill and people knowledge in a way that has made Apple computers a household name.

I believe there are thousands and thousands of technically talented people whose businesses would turn around overnight if only they mastered—or partnered with someone who possessed—people knowledge.

How would you describe "people knowledge"?

_____

_____

_____

2. Service Skills—Your Treatment of People Helps Build Your Business

Barry J. Gibbons, author of *This Indecision Is Final*, maintains, "Between 70 percent and 90 percent of decisions not to repeat a purchase of anything are not about product or price. They are about some dimension of the service relationship." Many businesses today recognize this fact, and as a result, they place greater emphasis on service to their customers. How you treat the people you do business with really matters, especially in a competitive marketplace. The more competitive the industry, the more important the service.

Under what circumstances would you choose to pay a higher price at one location for an item you could get for less at another store?

_____

_____

_____

3. Business Reputation—Your Reputation for Relationships Helps Build Your Business

Writer Howard Hodgson said, "Whatever business you are in, you are in a business of relationships. That's why your reputation is your greatest asset." Because of Bill Porter's physical disabilities, many people underestimated his people skills—until they got to know him. Porter knew how to connect with people and understand their needs. For that reason, he was a good salesman. He also conducted his business in such a way that his customers *always* got what they were promised, when it was promised. Over time, his reputation grew. And as a result, he has sold products to three and sometimes four generations of some families!

> *What percentage of the time do you deliver on your promises? How does this affect your relationships?*

_____

_____

_____

4. Personal Friendship—Your Friendship with Others Builds Your Business

The highest level of business relationships is reached when people like your business, but more importantly, when they like you! When there is a heart felt personal connection to another person, it becomes stronger than any other kind of business bond. That's why I say all things being equal, people will work with people they like; all things not being equal, they still will. Friendship is the difference-maker! Even when the odds are stacked against you, friendship many times will still give you the edge with the customer. Why? People like being and working with their friends.

> *List a few reasons you like to work with your friends. (If you don't enjoy working with friends, explore the reasons why. What might that say about you or the people you choose as friends?)*

_____

_____

_____

I read a story about the time when General William Westmoreland was in Vietnam, and he was reviewing a platoon of paratroopers. As he walked down the line, he asked each of them a question: "How do you like jumping, son?"

"Love it, sir!" was the first answer.

"The greatest experience in my life, sir!" exclaimed the next paratrooper.

But when he came to the third one, the soldier's response surprised him.

"I hate it, sir," the young man replied.

"Then why do you do it?" asked Westmoreland.

"Because I want to be around the guys who love to jump."

THE VALUE OF FRIENDSHIP

Although I've been examining the Friendship Principle solely in the context of business, it applies much more broadly. People want to engage in activities with people they like. Once again, this probably seems obvious, but I mention it because I want to emphasize the value—and power—of true friendship in every context and situation.

One person who had incredible insight about relationships was King Solomon of ancient Israel. It's said that he was the wisest person who ever lived. During the course of his lifetime, he wrote many wise things about friendships, and we can learn from them today. Here are a few of those truths about real friends:

Real Friends Are Scarce

Solomon wrote, "Friends come and friends go, but a true friend sticks by you like family."[2] When you develop a deep friendship with someone, value it because real friends are rare. A true friend . . .

is someone who sees you at your worst but never forgets your best.

is someone who thinks you're a little bit more wonderful than you really are.

is someone you can talk with for hours or be with in complete silence.

is as happy for your success as you are.

trusts you enough to say what he really means when talking to you.

doesn't try to know more, act smarter, or be your constant teacher.

In short, a real friend is a friend all the time.

Value the real friends you have. They are precious. More important, try to become a real friend to others. There are few gifts greater than being a friend.

What would you add to the above description of a "true friend"?

_____

_____

_____

Real Friends Are Refreshing

Solomon observed, "Just as lotions and fragrance give sensual delight, a sweet friendship refreshes the soul."[3] Every situation in life improves when a friend is involved. When you want to share a fun experience, there's nothing like having a friend with you. When you're facing a crisis, a friend shares its weight. C. S. Lewis said, "Friendship is born at the moment one person says to another, 'What, you, too? I thought I was the only one.'" That kind of connection is refreshing, no matter what's happening in your life.

How do others respond to you? When people see you coming, do they expect to be refreshed and energized? Or do they have to expend energy to sustain their interaction with you? Everyone should be a breath of fresh air to someone in his life.

Real Friends Make Us Better

In the best kinds of friendships, the people improve one another simply by being together. As Solomon said, "You use steel to sharpen steel, and one friend sharpens another."[4]

Automaker Henry Ford was having lunch with a person and asked him, "Who is your best friend?" As Ford waited for his response, the man hesitated. He wasn't sure.

"I will tell you who your best friend is," Ford jumped in. "Your best friend is the one who brings out the best that is within you."

That's what real friends do. They bring out each other's best.

How do your friends specifically make you better?

_____

_____

_____

Real Friends Remain Faithful

Have you heard this one? What do you get if you cross Lassie with a pit bull? You get a dog that bites your face off and then goes for help. Real friends aren't like that. In this world there are plenty of people who don't care about others. Solomon remarked, "Calloused climbers betray their very own friends; they'd stab their own grandmothers in the back."[5] But real friends remain faithful no matter what.

Author and pastor Richard Exley said, "A true friend is one who hears and understands when you share your deepest feelings. He supports you when you are struggling; he corrects you, gently and with love, when you err; and he forgives you when you fail. A true friend prods you to personal growth, stretches you to your full potential. And most amazing of all, he celebrates your successes as if they were his own."

APPLYING THE FRIENDSHIP PRINCIPLE DISCUSSION QUESTIONS

1. How can you tell when people place business ahead of friendship? How can you tell when they approach relationships the other way around? What motivates people to place business first? What motivates others to place friendship first? Which is your natural inclination?

_____

_____

_____

2. Do you agree that if you look at people in terms of friendship first and business second, then you have a chance of making a friend _and_ succeeding in business? Explain your answer.

_____

_____

_____

3. Consider the four levels of business relationships:

- People knowledge
- Personal friendship
- Business reputation
- Service skills

On what level are most of the people you do business with? Does it matter whether the person is a colleague or client? Where would you like them to be? What is preventing you from taking your business relationships to the next level?

_____

_____

_____

4. Have you ever worked in a company or industry with a bad business reputation? What was it like? Is it possible to practice the Friendship Principle in such an environment? What kinds of things work against you in such a situation? What must you do to succeed and practice the Friendship Principle?

_____

_____

_____

5. Do you agree that true friends are people who bring out the best in you? If so, how does that work? Do people who bring out your best _become_ your friends? Or because people _are_ your friends, they bring out your best? How do the encouragement from and sharpening by friends apply in the work environment?

_____

_____

_____

Summary

You cannot sustain a deep friendship with everyone, nor should you try. But you should cultivate genuine deep friendships with a few people. And you can be a friendly, kind, supportive person to everyone you meet. You can treat every person as an individual, not simply a business "contact." If you put others first as people and then worry about business second, you're on your way to practicing the Friendship Principle.

No matter what kind of business or industry you're in, the Friendship Principle can help you. It doesn't matter if you're the salesman or the customer, a boss or an employee, an executive or a stay-at-home mom. Whatever work you do, people will be more inclined to do it with you when you treat them like friends.

THE PARTNERSHIP PRINCIPLE

Working Together Increases the Odds of Winning Together

You can do what I cannot do. I can do what you cannot do.
Together we can do great things.

—MOTHER TERESA

THE QUESTION I MUST ASK MYSELF:
ARE OTHERS BETTER OFF BECAUSE OF
THEIR PARTNERSHIP WITH ME?

S ome people just naturally approach life with a partnership mind-set. And as a result, they reap unusual success. Benjamin Franklin was one such person.

Franklin is remembered as a printer, statesman, inventor, writer, and founding father of the United States. He was born in Boston, the fifteenth of seventeen children, the son of a candle maker. His formal schooling lasted less than two years. At age twelve, he apprenticed to his brother to learn the trade of printing. At seventeen with no resources other than his talent and hard work, he moved to Philadelphia to seek his fortune, starting out as a printer and journalist. By 1730, at age twenty-four, he owned his own business. In 1748, he was wealthy enough to retire.

The reason Franklin wanted to retire was to devote himself to scientific research. His experiments with electricity made him world famous. Beginning in the 1750s, he became heavily involved in community affairs and politics. Once again, his accomplishments were incredible. He was one of a handful of influencers who shaped the American Revolution and the creation of the new country. A cowriter of the Declaration of Independence and the Constitution, he is the only person to have signed the four documents that helped to create the United States: the Declaration of Independence (1776), the Treaty of Alliance, Amity, and Commerce with France (1778), the Treaty of Peace between England, France, and the United States (1782), and the Constitution (1787).[1]

PARTNERSHIP MAKER

A quick review of Franklin's accomplishments might tempt one to believe that Franklin was the kind of person inclined to work alone. Nothing could be farther from the truth. Franklin embraced the Partnership Principle from early in his career. Despite his meager education, Franklin was a lifelong learner. But he knew his greatest progress would not come working alone. So in 1727, at the age of twenty-one, he founded a group called the Junto. Franklin described it as "a club of mutual improvement" composed of "most of my ingenious acquaintances." The original group included printers, surveyors, craftsmen, a clerk, and a merchant. "We met on Fridays," Franklin said. "The rules that I drew up required that every member, in his turn, should produce one or more queries on any point of Morals, Politics, or Natural

Philosophy, to be discuss'd by the company; and once in three months produce and read an essay of his own writing, on any subject he pleased."[2] Franklin's Junto eventually evolved into the American Philosophical Society, which still exists today.

An important part of Franklin's continuing self-education was reading books. Often short of funds when he was young, Franklin came up with a partnership approach to acquiring books. He convinced a group of people to pool their money and buy a library of books to be shared. By 1731, the idea evolved into the nation's first lending library.

Franklin used a similar partnership approach again and again. Because of the threat of fire in Philadelphia, he convinced a group of colonists to come together to form the city's first volunteer firefighting club in 1736. In the event of a fire threatening the property of any club member, all of the other members would come to his aid. In 1751, he helped to found the first public hospital in the country. In 1752, he encouraged a group of colonists to share financial risks by partnering in the Philadelphia Contributorship, America's first fire insurance company. He got people to work together to hire street sweepers and to employ local policemen. Time after time, Franklin teamed up with others so that all could achieve success.

No matter how successful Franklin became, he never abandoned his partnership approach to achievement. He employed it on national and international scales. When the United States was seeking its independence, its founders knew that the country would not survive without the help and partnership of other nations. Franklin was dispatched to Europe as the nation's first minister to France. He was successful in persuading the French to partner with America against the British. Scholar Leo Lemay called Franklin "the most essential and successful American diplomat of all time".[3]

And after the young nation had secured its independence and was attempting to write its constitution in 1787, when delegates could not agree on the structure of the legislature, Franklin proposed the "great compromise" that created our current two-house congressional structure. Few men have had a greater impact on the United States. And few people have understood the power of partnership the way Franklin did.

LEARNING TO LOOK TO OTHERS

From his youth, Ben Franklin understood that working together increases the odds of winning together. I wish I had been as wise. It took me a long time to learn the Partnership Principle. In this area of life, I have gone through four stages:

1. I Want to Make a Difference . . .

Like many people, I started out in what I call the self stage. My focus was on me and what I could do. That's not to say I was doing anything wrong. My motives were positive. It's just that my perspective—along with my effectiveness—was so limited. I worked hard, and I got a lot done. But I couldn't do anything of real significance by myself. What I later discovered and wrote in *The 17 Irrefutable Laws of Teamwork* is really true: one is too small a number to achieve greatness.

> *Do you agree with the statement: "one is too small a number to achieve greatness"? Explain.*

_____

_____

_____

My personal definition of *high morale* is "I make a difference." Conversely my definition of *low morale* is "I make no difference at all." If your personal sense of well-being is affected by your ability to make a positive impact on others, then you need to think beyond what only you can do.

2. I Want to Make a Difference with People . . .

When I began to look beyond myself, I discovered that I could go farther and achieve more when others joined me on the journey. As a result, I wanted to take *everybody* with me. It didn't take me long to realize that was a mistake. Here's why:

- *Not everyone* should *take the trip—passion*. Have you ever worked with people who said they were on board with you and believed in what you were trying to accomplish, yet you kept having to talk them into doing their part? Those people have no passion for the work. They may want to take the ride, but they have no interest in pedaling. Take them on, and they will wear you out.

- *Not everyone* wants *to take the trip—attitude*. Some people simply don't believe in you or what you're doing. That doesn't mean you're wrong, nor does it make them wrong. It just means you shouldn't try to take them with you.

- *Not everyone* can *take the trip—ability*. The difference between a partnership and a rescue mission is capacity. Some people may want to make a difference, but they have no ability to affect what you're doing. You cannot afford to partner with someone with whom there is no fit.

The main lesson I learned during this phase is that I should try to build relationships with everyone, but I should forge partnerships with only a few.

What makes a relationship a partnership?

_____

_____

_____

3. I Want to Make a Difference with People Who Want to Make a Difference . . .

English statesman Henry Van Dyke observed, "In the progress of personality, first comes a declaration of independence, then a recognition of interdependence." When I turned forty, I entered a season of life where I finally started to realize this truth: those closest to you determine your level of success. It was then that I moved from simply working with good, capable people to partnering with difference makers. And let me tell you the secret of going to the next level in this area: find capable people with the same passion and mission as yours who also need others to make a difference. When you create partnerships with these people, there's no telling what you can do together.

What is your passion and/or mission? Where will you look to find people with your same passion and mission? How can you partner with them?

_____

_____

_____

4. I Want to Make a Difference with People Who Want to Make a Difference Doing Something that Makes a Difference

Only at this time of my life have I entered what I call the significance stage. I have many rewarding relational partnerships, and together we are doing many things that are making a positive impact by helping others. I can't imagine anything more rewarding.

Rabbi Harold Kushner remarked, "The purpose of life is not to win. The purpose of life is to grow and to share. When you come to look back on all that you have done in life, you will get more satisfaction from the pleasure you have brought into other people's lives than you will from the times that you outdid and defeated them."

What are you doing to grow and share? How do other people factor into your efforts?

_____

_____

_____

THE POWER OF PARTNERSHIP

As you read the previous pages, you may have noticed something about the progression I experienced:

> I want to make a difference (self stage) . . .
> with people who want to make a difference (sharing stage) . . .
> doing something that makes a difference (significance stage)!

Between the self stage and the significance stage was the discovery of the sharing stage with people. Incredible power comes from partnership with others. It can be one of the most rewarding experiences of life. It has so many benefits:

When You Partner with Others, You Lose Nothing

Thomas Jefferson observed, "A candle loses nothing when it lights another candle." That is the real nature of partnership. I find that many people don't think that way. They believe that sharing means losing something. But I don't think that's true.

Every person possesses one of two mind-sets: scarcity or abundance. People with a scarcity mind-set believe that there's only so much to go around, so you have to scrap for everything you can and protect whatever you have at all costs. People with an abundance mind-set believe there's always enough to go around. If you have an idea, share it; you can always come up with another one. If you have money, give some of it away; you can always make more. If you have only one piece of pie, let someone else eat it; you can bake another one.

I believe that in this area, you get from life what you expect. You can hoard what little you have and receive no more. Or you can give what you have, and you will be rewarded with abundance. Your attitude makes the difference. So if you partner with another person and give generously, one way or another you're going to get back more than you gave.

Looking back on your childhood, did your parents display a scarcity or abundance mindset? How did this affect your family?

_____

_____

_____

When You Partner with Others, You Help Yourself

Novelist Mark Twain said, "The best way to cheer yourself up is to cheer everybody else up." What he knew instinctively was that when you help others, you help yourself. At the very least, you will receive the satisfaction of helping another human being. But more likely than not, when you help other people, they desire to turn around and help you.

Richard Shipley, president and CEO of Shipley Associates, offers this advice: "Work well with others to help them achieve their own victories; yours will follow. Share ownership with the right people. You'll spend many hours with these colleagues, so select associates you really enjoy working with. Allow successful colleagues to share the equity in your mutual efforts."

When You Partner with Others, You Are Rewarded with Hope

In 2003 Dave Sutherland, who had been the president of one of my companies, INJOY Stewardship Services (ISS), was ready to make a transition and move to the West Coast where his children and grandchildren live. Dave had done a wonderful job of building the company for almost a decade, and I wondered how I was going to replace him. It didn't take me long to realize who needed to succeed him in leading the company: Kirk Nowery.

Kirk, a former pastor, had come aboard years before at ISS and had worked with hundreds of pastors and churches. He has a passion for adding value to pastors, his skills are tremendous, and no one has worked harder. And he is an excellent leader. I couldn't think of anyone I'd rather partner with in helping churches fulfill their vision. So Margaret and I talked with Kirk, and after several lengthy discussions, I offered him the job.

A few days later, Margaret and I got a card in the mail. The printed message read, "For all that has been, Thanks. For all that will be, Yes.—Dag Hammarskjold." Below it Kirk had handwritten,

Dear John and Margaret, with the deepest respect and honor, I accept.

That moment brought me great joy, and I was so grateful. Why? Because I knew that the future of ISS was bright.

APPLYING THE PARTNERSHIP PRINCIPLE

1. What does "making a difference" mean to you? Have you considered whether or how you desire to make a difference in your lifetime? What is your dream? What steps must you take to accomplish it?

_____

_____

_____

2. In what stage are most of the people you know: the self stage, the people stage, or the significance stage? How can you tell? Must everyone go through the first two before entering the third? What stage are you in currently? Explain your answer.

_____

_____

_____

3. How much control do you have over the people you work with most closely? Does that make an impact on your ability to achieve your goals and fulfill your dreams? If you have little control, what could you do to change that situation? In what areas could you currently surround yourself with make-a-difference people? How can you go about finding people with the same passion, a similar mission, talent, and a need for partnership?

_____

_____

_____

4. Describe a marriage that functions as a true partnership. What are the advantages of such a relationship? What happens when marriage partners don't work together? If you are married, describe your attitude toward matrimonial partnership. Describe your spouse's. What can the two of you do to increase your ability to work together?

_____

_____

_____

5. Should leaders try to cultivate relational partnerships with people who work with them? Explain. If so, when would that be appropriate? If you are a leader, what kinds of people have you surrounded yourself with? Do you think of those closest to you as working *with* you or working *for* you? What, if anything, would you like to change in how you interact with them?

_____

_____

_____

Summary

If you desire to cultivate win-win relationships, embrace the Partnership Principle. You probably know in your heart that what you can do alone pales in comparison to what you can do with others. Self-made men (and women) don't make very much. The most rewarding relationships are always partnerships. I've found that it's true in business, it's true in marriage, and I believe it will be true for you.

THE SATISFACTION PRINCIPLE

In Great Relationships,
the Joy of Being Together Is Enough

A joy shared is a joy doubled.

—Johann Wolfgang von Goethe

THE QUESTION I MUST ASK MYSELF:
DO MY CLOSEST FRIENDS
ENJOY JUST BEING WITH ME?

During the fourteen years that I led my church in San Diego, every December we put on a big charity show to reach the community and raise money for a local child abuse foundation. I always participated, acting as master of ceremonies and sometimes doing a comic cameo in one of the scenes. Most years we did at least twenty-four performances. It was an exhilarating, yet exhausting, experience.

Before every performance, I used to go out and warm up the crowd by talking to everyone and interacting with the audience. One of the things I liked to do was to find the couple in the audience who had been married the longest. I still remember the one couple who held the record from all the years I did it. They had been married seventy-seven years!

As the couple stood and the audience applauded for them, their eyes sparkled.

"Do you want me to give you two marriage counseling?" I asked, getting a quick laugh from the audience.

The old gentleman looked at me, smiled, and said almost confidentially, "It just gets better and better."

THE GREATEST SATISFACTION

Most of us admire and respect people who sustain solid, long-term relationships. A marriage of more than seventy-five years is remarkable. And friendships of any kind that last for decades are the envy of many.

One of the great friendships in Hollywood, a city that is often criticized for its superficiality, was developed between George Burns and Jack Benny. Burns's thirty-eight-year marriage to Gracie Allen (until her death in 1964) was admirable. But his friendship with Jack Benny lasted even longer. After Benny's death in 1976, Burns characterized their relationship this way:

Jack and I had a wonderful friendship for nearly fifty-five years. Jack never walked out on me while I sang a song, and I never walked out on him while he played the violin. We laughed together, we played together, we worked together, we ate together. I suppose that for many of those years we talked every single day.

I think all of us would love to have a relationship like that of Benny and Burns or like that of an older married couple we've met. But how do we get there? The foundation is built upon all the previous People Principles in this book. A lasting relationship begins as a healthy relationship. Beyond that, I believe that four factors help to create the right climate for relationships where simply being together is enough:

1. Shared Memories Create a Bonded Environment

In March 2004, Margaret and I took a seventeen-day trip to Africa with EQUIP, the nonprofit organization I founded to teach leadership to people overseas. It was a grueling trip. We traveled long distances to four different countries on the continent. Many mornings we were up teaching by seven o'clock, and we went nonstop until midnight or 1:00 A.M. During those two and a half weeks of teaching, we had only one break. We took a two-day safari to see the magnificent wildlife of the bush country.

One person who accompanied us on this trip was Tom Mullins. Tom is a good leader and highly successful pastor of a large church in Florida, and he was helping the team with the teaching responsibilities. Tom and I have been friends for about eight years, and the longer I know him, the deeper my respect and affection for him have become.

The afternoon we got home to Atlanta from Africa, Margaret and I dragged ourselves home from the airport and went to bed. All we wanted to do was sleep. Even the next day, we were still jet-lagged and worn out. As I sat at my desk sorting through mail and catching up on work, I got a phone call. It was Tom. It had been only a day since we'd seen each other, but already he wanted to reminisce. We laughed about our safari. (The other tourists came loaded with expensive cameras with zoom lenses, while Tom and I were armed with nothing but a disposable camera!) We recalled the difficult travel. And we marveled at the response of the thousands of people we taught.

"John," Tom finally said, "let's do it again!" Tom and I will never forget that trip together. And the memories we share will forever provide a common bond between us.

Those kinds of experiences are invaluable in our deepest relationships. Margaret and I tried to create many memories with our children as they were growing up. And from the time we got married, we vowed that we would do whatever it took so that when we created our greatest memories, we would be together.

Think of your closest relationship. What memories or key experiences do you share with that person?

_____

_____

_____

2. Growing Together Creates a Committed Environment

Back in the 1970s when we lived in Lancaster, Ohio, Margaret and I became involved in our first business. She and two friends decided that they wanted to become partners and open a floral shop. We didn't have any money in those days, so we created a business plan and talked to a local banker about a loan. I still vividly remember sitting across from him in his office.

"There's good news and bad news," he said. "The good news is that I'm going to give you the loan." We were elated. "The bad news is that if you're like most new business owners, your partnership will break up in a couple of years. Many start together; few stay together."

That can be said of all kinds of relationships. Beginnings and endings are often much easier than the hard work of sustaining a relationship. Why?

> Beginning relationships possess the _excitement_ of _starting_ together.
> Continuing relationships possess the _commitment_ of _sticking_ together.
> Lasting relationships possess the _joy_ of _staying_ together.

So what is the bridge that spans the gap between relationships that start together and those that stay together? The answer is growth. People who grow together become more committed to one another. And they are usually happier, too.

In truth, all relationships grow—they grow apart or they grow together. If we are intentional about growing together, then we are much likelier to stay together. Unfortunately what the banker told us back in Lancaster turned out to be true. By the end of the second year, one of the partners was no longer committed to the business and bowed out.

How do you and your spouse or closest friend grow together?

_____

_____

_____

3. Mutual Respect Creates a Healthy Environment

Respect is usually earned during difficult times, and respect within a relationship creates a healthy environment because it produces two things. First, it creates trust, and as you know, trust is the foundation of all relationships. Second, it engenders servanthood. People almost can't stop themselves from helping and serving someone they deeply respect. And as Albert Einstein said, "Only a life lived for others is worthwhile."

Would you agree that the cause of most divorces can be traced back to a lack of mutual respect? Explain.

_____

_____

_____

4. Unconditional Love Creates a Safe Environment

Children's author Dinah Maria Mulock Craik wrote, "Oh, the inexpressible comfort of feeling safe with a person; having neither to weigh thoughts nor measure words, but to pour them all out, just as they are, chaff and grain together, knowing that a faithful hand will take and sift them, keep what is worth keeping, and then, with the breath of kindness, blow the rest away." When somebody loves you with no strings attached and no personal agenda, it's the most freeing thing in the world. It creates a safe environment wherever you are.

Recently Margaret and I were traveling together on a plane, and we struck up a conversation with another couple seated across the aisle from us. When the woman asked, "Where's home?" without even thinking, I said, "Wherever she is," pointing to my wife. And that's true. Margaret loves me unconditionally. I can be myself with her like I am with no other person in the world. She is my safe harbor. There is nothing sweeter in this life than the unconditional love of your closest friend.

I feel very fortunate to have Margaret. I tell people all the time that the greatest decision I ever made was to ask her to marry me. I think about that daily. And I try to tell her as often as I can. On Valentine's Day 2004, I wrote her a note reflecting on our relationship. She has given me permission to share it with you:

Margaret,
It was about this time forty years ago that we started dating. Although each year seems to be going by quicker than the previous one, our lives have been filled with memories. At

fifty-six, I have forgotten many, but the special ones are still today very real to me. I ask myself, "Were the memories special because of what we did or because we experienced them together?" The answer is . . . both. The specialness was greater because we were together.

When we are apart I look forward to our telephone time each evening. It's the highlight of my day. Why? Is it because we both share our list of things that have happened to us that day? No. It is because we are once again together.

I can well remember the anticipation I felt when we were courting as I drove from Circleville to Chillicothe for a date night with you. I could hardly wait! The years have not diminished the anticipation to once again see you after I have been gone. That's why I call you as I leave the airport on my way home. Margaret, the joy you display when you see me again has stayed strong over all these years. Each time I call, you answer the phone with an excitement that expresses to me that I am loved.

I'll never forget the time you sold some of your Ohio State textbooks and bought a bus ticket so you could surprise me and we could have an evening together. Or the time you traveled from Nepal to Delhi to spend an extra night with me. Those extra efforts to be together are what have made our marriage so successful.

A relationship never stays the same. It either grows closer or apart. Forty years after ours began, we still like to be together. Let's take a walk to the mailbox.

Love,

John

Taking a walk to the mailbox for us means spending time together just for the joy of it. And that's what all great relationships provide. Joy.

Applying the Satisfaction Principle

1. Can a person be standoffish and still develop a rewarding win-win relationship? Explain your answer. What is the price a person has to pay to develop deep relationships? What would make the price worth paying for you?

_____

_____

_____

2. Think about people you know personally who have sustained a good relationship for more than twenty years. (It can be any kind of relationship,

such as a married couple, business partners, or friends.) Describe their relationship. What do they do to keep the relationship going? What can you learn from them?

_____

_____

_____

3. In relationships with a high degree of safety, how do mutual respect and unconditional love come into play? Think about the closest relationship in your life. Do you feel safe with that person? Can you say anything you want? Can you express your feelings? Are you comfortable with long silences? If not, how can you change the environment and make it more positive?

_____

_____

_____

4. Describe some ways that married couples can grow together to make sure that they do not grow apart. How difficult is it to make growth part of a marriage? What challenges or obstacles do most couples face? How can they overcome them? What is the reward of perseverance? Have you succeeded in this area in your marriage?

_____

_____

_____

5. How intentional are you about creating new memories with your family or close friends? How can you improve in this area?

_____

_____

_____

Summary

I hope you have people in your life with whom you can share the Satisfaction Principle. If you do, be grateful. If you don't, then begin by practicing the People Principles in this book. Then cultivate rewarding relationships where you create shared memories, grow together, and give each other mutual respect and unconditional love. Do that, and it's only a matter of time before you experience the joy that comes from deep, long-lasting relationships.

FINAL REVIEW OF THE PEOPLE PRINCIPLES FOR WINNING WITH PEOPLE

THE READINESS QUESTION— ARE WE PREPARED FOR RELATIONSHIPS?

The Lens Principle: Who we are determines how we view others.

The Mirror Principle: The first person we must examine is ourselves.

The Pain Principle: Hurting people hurt people and are easily hurt by them.

The Hammer Principle: Never use a hammer to swat a fly off someone's head.

The Elevator Principle: We can lift people up or take people down in our relationships.

THE CONNECTION QUESTION— ARE WE WILLING TO FOCUS ON OTHERS?

The Big Picture Principle: The entire population of the world—with one minor exception—is composed of others.

The Exchange Principle: Instead of putting others in their place, we must put ourselves in their place.

The Learning Principle: Each person we meet has the potential to teach us something.

The Charisma Principle: People are interested in the person who is interested in them.

The Number 10 Principle: Believing the best in people usually brings the best out of people.

The Confrontation Principle: Caring for people should precede confronting people.

THE TRUST QUESTION— CAN WE BUILD MUTUAL TRUST?

The Bedrock Principle: Trust is the foundation of any relationship.

The Situation Principle: Never let the situation mean more than the relationship.

The Bob Principle: When Bob has a problem with everyone, Bob is usually the problem.

The Approachability Principle: Being at ease with ourselves helps others be at ease with us.

The Foxhole Principle: When preparing for battle, dig a hole big enough for a friend.

THE INVESTMENT QUESTION— ARE WE WILLING TO INVEST IN OTHERS?

The Gardening Principle: All relationships need cultivation.

The 101 Percent Principle: Find the 1 percent we agree on and give it 100 percent of our effort.

The Patience Principle: The journey with others is slower than the journey alone.

The Celebration Principle: The true test of relationships is not only how loyal we are when friends fail, but how thrilled we are when they succeed.

The High Road Principle: We go to a higher level when we treat others better than they treat us.

THE SYNERGY QUESTION—
CAN WE CREATE A WIN-WIN RELATIONSHIP?

The Boomerang Principle: When we help others, we help ourselves.

The Friendship Principle: All things being equal, people will work with people they like; all things not being equal, they still will.

The Partnership Principle: Working together increases the odds of winning together.

The Satisfaction Principle: In great relationships, the joy of being together is enough.

NOTES

Introduction

1. Zig Ziglar, *Top Performance: How to Develop Excellence in Yourself and Others* (New York: Berkley Publishing Group, 1991), italics added.

The Mirror Principle

1. "Pete's Records," www.peterose.com (accessed 20 January 2004).

2. Pete Rose, www.baseball-reference.com (accessed 20 January 2004).

3. Jill Lieber and Craig Neff, "The Case Against Pete Rose," *Sports Illustrated*, 5 January 2004, www.si.cnn.com (accessed 15 January 2004).

4. Rose, www.baseball-reference.com (accessed 20 January 2004).

5. "Pete Rose: 'I bet on baseball,'" excerpt from *My Prison Without Bars*, in *Sports Illustrated*, 5 January 2004, www.si.com.

6. Craig Neff and Jill Lieber, "Rose's Grim Vigil," *Sports Illustrated*, 3 April 1989, www.si.cnn.com (accessed 5 January 2004).

7. Jill Lieber and Craig Neff, "The Case Against Pete Rose," *Sports Illustrated*, 3 July 1989, www.si.cnn.com (accessed 15 January 2004).

8. "Pete Rose: 'I bet on baseball.'"

9. Ibid.

10. Ibid.

The Hammer Principle

1. Proverbs 15:1.

2. Marshall Goldsmith, "How to Learn the Truth About Yourself," *Fast Company*, October 2003, 127.

The Elevator Principle

1. George W. Crane, *Dr. Crane's Radio Talks*, vol. 1 (Mellot, IN: Hopkis Syndicate, Inc., 1948), 7.

2. Ibid., 8, 9.

3. Ibid., 16.

4. Anonymous.

The Big Picture Principle

1. "Meet the New Angelina Jolie," www.cnn.com/2003/showbiz/movies/10/25/jolie.ap (accessed 13 January 2004).

2. "Child Changes Everything," ABCNews.com, 17 October 2003.

3. Ibid.

4. Ibid.

5. Ibid.

6. "Meet the New Angelina Jolie."

7. Joke Distribution Network.

8. Anonymous.

The Exchange Principle

1. Art Mortell, "How to Master the Inner Game of Selling," vol. 10, no. 7.

The Learning Principle

1. Tom Seligson, "How a Wiseguy Set Me Straight," *Parade*, 18 January 2004, 18.

2. Ibid.

3. Joe Pantoliano with David Evanier, *Who's Sorry Now* (New York: Plume, 2002), 243.

4. Ibid., 14.

5. Ibid., 289.

6. Philip B. Crosby, *Quality Is Free: The Art of Making Quality Certain* (New York: Mentor Books, 1992), 68.

The Number 10 Principle

1. Marilyn Haddrill, "Lessons in Learning: Ex-Marine-turned-teacher Shapes up her Tough High School Class," *Chicago Tribune*, 3 March 1996, http://internet.cybermesa.com (accessed 22 January 2004).

2. Ibid.

3. Ibid.

4. LouAnne Johnson, *The Girls in the Back of the Class* (New York: St. Martin's Press, 1995), 61.

5. LouAnne Johnson, *Dangerous Minds* (New York: St. Martin's Press, 1993), 7.

6. Johnson, *The Girls in the Back of the Class*, ix, x.

7. Haddrill, "Lessons in Learning."

8. LouAnne Johnson, "My Posse Don't Do Homework," http://members.authorsguild.net/louanne/work4.htm (accessed 22 January 2004).

The Bedrock Principle

1. Dan Barry, David Barstow, Jonathan D. Glater, Adam Liptak, and Jacques Steinberg, "Correcting the Record: Times Reporter Who Resigned Leaves Long Trail of Deception," *New York Times*, 11 May 2003, http://query.nytimes.com (accessed 9 March 2004).

2. Elizabeth Kolbert, "Tumult in the Newsroom," *New Yorker*, 30 June 2003, www.newyorker.com (accessed 9 March 2004).

3. Barry et al., "Correcting the Record."

4. Paul D. Colford, "More Blair Faults at Times," *New York Daily News*, 13 June 2003, www.nydailynews.com (accessed 9 March 2004).

5. Barry et al., "Correcting the Record."

6. Peter Johnson, "'Times' Execs Address Blair Scandal," *USA Today*, 14 May 2003, http://usatoday.printthis.clickability.com (accessed 9 March 2004).

7. Barry et al., "Correcting the Record."

8. Ibid.

9 Macarena Hernandez, "What Jayson Blair Stole from Me, and Why I Couldn't Ignore It," *Washington Post*, 1 June 2003, www.washingtonpost.com (accessed 9 March 2004).

10. "Burning Down My Master's House: My Life at *The New York Times*," *Publishers Weekly*, 8 March 2004, 58.

11. "Numbers," *Time*, 29 March 2004, 19.

12. Barry et al., "Correcting the Record."

13. John C. Maxwell, *The 21 Irrefutable Laws of Leadership* (Nashville: Thomas Nelson, 1998).

14. D. Michael Abrashoff, *It's Your Ship* (New York: Warner Business, 2002), 65.

The Situation Principle

1. "Willams Sisters Display Loving Sibling Rivalry at Australian Open," *Jet*, 9 February 1998, www.findarticles.com (accessed 5 February 2004).

2. L. Jon Wertheim, "We Told You So," *Sports Illustrated*, 5 April 1999, http://sportsillustrated.cnn.com (accessed 4 February 2004).

3. Timeline: Venus and Serena Williams, http://sportsillustrated.cnn.com/tennis/features/williams/timeline (accessed 4 February 2004).

4. Wertheim, "We Told You So."

The Bob Principle

1. Tobias Seamon, "The All-Bastard Athletic Club," *The Morning News*, 10 June 2002, www.themorningnews.org/archives/personalities (accessed 28 January 2004).

2. *Sports Illustrated*, 30 March 1981, quoted on http://espn.go.com/classic/s/quotesbmartin000806.html (accessed 23 January 2004).

3. Ibid.

4. Interview, *New York Times*, 15 July 1982.

The Approachability Principle

1. "Biography of Barbara Walters," us.imdb.com/name/nm0910181/bio (accessed 19 February 2004).

2. Tina Gianoulis, "Barbara Walters," *St. James Encyclopedia of Popular Culture*, 2002, www.findarticles.com (accessed 17 February 2004).

3. Ibid.

4. Alberta Civil Service Association *News*.

5. Florence Littauer, *Personality Plus: How to Understand Others By Understanding Yourself* (Grand Rapids, MI: Fleming H. Revell, 2003).

6. *Simpson's Contemporary Quotations*.

7. Barbara Walters, *How to Talk with Practically Anybody About Practically Anything* (Garden City, NY: Doubleday, 1970), xv.

The Foxhole Principle

1. *Army Field Manual* number 7–8, Headquarters, Department of the Army, Washington, DC, 22 April 1992, www.adtdl.army.mil/cgi-bin/atdl.dll/fm/7-8/ch2.htm#s2p6 (accessed 17 March 2004).

2. Ecclesiastes 4:9–12.

3. Tom and David Gardner, "Motley Fool Radio Interview with Yahoo! Co-Founder Jerry Yang," www.fool.com/Specials/1999/sp990303YangInterview.htm (accessed 11 March 2004).

4. Jon Swartz, "Yahoo's Other Dynamic Duo: Jeff Mallett and Tim Koogle Have Transformed the Service into the Web's Most Popular Site," *San Francisco Chronicle*, 6 August 1998, www.sfgate.com (accessed 12 March 2004).

5. Http://docs.yahoo.com/info/pr/faq.html (accessed 12 March 2004.)

6. Robert Lauer and Jeanette Lauer, *Watersheds* (Boston: Little, Brown, 1988), 69.

The Gardening Principle

1. "Mitch Albom Bio," www.albom.com (accessed 11 March 2004).

2. Tracy Cochran, "Everyone Matters," *Publishers Weekly*, 18 August 2003, www.publishersweekly.com (accessed 12 March 2004).

3. Mitch Albom, "He Was a Champion," *Parade*, 14 September 2003, 4, 5.

4. Ibid., 4.

5. Cochran, "Everyone Matters."

6. Albom, "He Was a Champion," 5.

7. Ibid.

The 101 Percent Principle

1. Laura Hillenbrand, *Seabiscuit: An American Legend* (New York: Random House, 2001), 29.

2. Ibid., 33, 34.

The Patience Principle

1. "Lawn Chair Larry: 1982 Honorable Mention," www.darwinawards.com/stupid/stupid1997-11c.html (accessed 10 February 2004).

2. Warren G. Bennis and Burt Nanus, *Leaders: The Strategies for Taking Charge* (New York: HarperBusiness, 1985), 52.

The High Road Principle

1. Richard Collier, *The General Next to God: The Story of William Booth and the Salvation Army* (London: Collins Clear-Type Press, 1965), 27.

2. Steve Artus, "General William Booth—Salvation Army," *Claves Regni*, October 1994, www.stpetersnottingham.org (accessed 25 February 2004).

3. "William Booth," www.spartacus.schoolnet.co.uk/rebooth.htm (accessed 25 February 2004).

4. "The Founder–William Booth," http://archive.salvationarmy.org.uk (accessed 25 February 2004).

5. Collier, *The General Next to God*, 110.

6. "The Skeleton Army," www1.salvationarmy.org/heritage.nsf (accessed 15 March 2004).

7. "History," www.salvationarmyusa.org (accessed 25 February 2004).

8. Artus, "General William Booth—Salvation Army."

The Boomerang Principle

1. Alan Loy McGinnis, *The Friendship Factor* (Minneapolis: Augsburg Fortress, 1979).

The Friendship Principle

1. Bethany Broadwell, "Bill Porter: Selling His Uplifting Attitude," 9 August 2002, www.ican.com/news/fullpage.dfm (accessed 4 March 1004).

2. Proverbs 18:24 *The Message*.

3. Proverbs 27:9 *The Message*.

4. Proverbs 27:17 *The Message*.

5. Proverbs 16:28 *The Message*.

The Partnership Principle

1. "Ben Franklin As a Founding Father," http://sln.fi.edu/franklin/statsman/statsman (accessed 1 March 2004).

2. "Ben Franklin: Networker," www.pbs.org/benfranklin/13 citizen networker.html (accessed 1 March 2004).

3. "Ben Franklin: France," www.pbs.org/benfranklin/13 citizen france.html (accessed 1 March 2004).

4. Anonymous.

ABOUT THE AUTHOR

John C. Maxwell, known as America's expert on leadership, speaks in person to hundreds of thousands of people each year. He has communicated his leadership principles to Fortune 500 companies, the United States Military Academy at West Point, and sports organizations such as the NCAA, the NBA, and the NFL.

Maxwell is the founder of several organizations, including Maximum Impact, dedicated to helping people reach their leadership potential. He is the author of more than thirty books, including *Developing the Leader Within You, Your Road Map for Success*, and the *New York Times* best-selling *The 21 Irrefutable Laws of Leadership*, which has sold more than one million copies.

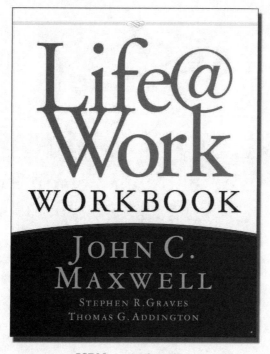

NELSON IMPACT
A Division of Thomas Nelson Publishers
Since 1798

The Nelson Impact Team is here to answer your questions
and suggestions as to how we can create more resources
that benefit you, your family, and your community.

Contact us at Impact@thomasnelson.com